Sea Life GAMES & PUZZLES

100 Brainteasers, Word Games, Jokes & Riddles,
Picture Puzzles, Matches, & Logic Tests

Cindy A. Littlefield

Illustrations by Michael Kline, Greg Wenzel, and Carol Maglitta

Storey Publishing

*The mission of Storey Publishing is to serve our customers by
publishing practical information that encourages
personal independence in harmony with the environment.*

Edited by Nancy D. Wood
Cover and text, design and production by one[visual]mind
Cover photograph © Digital Vision/Getty
Cover illustrations © Michael Kline
Interior illustrations © Michael Kline: ii, iii, v, vi, 1, 2, 4-5, 6 top, 8 top, 9–10, 12–13, 14 top, 16–17, 18 top,
22–26, 26, 28, 30–31, 33–34, 3 top, 38, 42–43, 45, 55 top, 56–58, 60–64, 66 top, 68–69, 74 top, 80–81,
84–85, 86 bottom right, 87 bottom two, 88 top, 89, 90 bottom, 91 middle, 92, 93 bottom left, 94 top, 95,
96 top, 97 bottom, 98 top, 99, 115; © Carol Maglitta: iv, 17 bottom, 22 top, 26 bottom, 28 bottom, 33 bottom,
38–39 bottom, 40–41, 44, 46–48, 51–55, 59 bottom, 61 bottom, 63 bottom, 66–67, 69 bottom, 77–79, 83,
90 middle, 91 bottom, 93 bottom right, 94 bottom, 97 middle, 98 bottom, 100, 103, 104, 106, 110, 112;
© Greg Wenzel: 3, 6, 7–8, 11, 14–15, 20–21, 27, 29 top, 32, 35, 39, 50 bottom, 59, 65, 72–73, 75, 76–77,
82, 86 top & bottom left, 87 top, 88 bottom two, 89 bottom, 90 top, 91 top, 93 top, 96 bottom two, 97 top,
98 middle.
Expert Review by Edward Seidel, Tenji, Inc.

Text © 2006 by Cindy A. Littlefield

The information in this book is true and complete to the best of our knowledge. All recommendations
are made without guarantee on the part of the author or Storey Publishing. The author and publisher
disclaim any liability in connection with the use of this information. For additional information please
contact Storey Publishing, 210 MASS MoCA Way, North Adams, MA 01247.

Storey books are available for special premium and promotional uses and for customized editions.
For further information, please call 1-800-793-9396.

Printed in the United States by Malloy
10 9 8 7 6 5

I dedicate this book to my son, Ian,

who can glide through the water

with confidence and ease, and has

never shied away from swimming

against the tide.

HEY KIDS! You might be smart, but you can't know everything! If a puzzle has you stumped, check out the definitions in the back of this book. Also, I'll pop up every now and then with a hint. Good luck, and have fun!

Contents

Introduction

All aboard and welcome, landlubbers! The Puzzle Lovers' Sea Life Sightseeing Cruise is about to begin. We're sure you're eager to get under way, but before we leave the dock, here are a few announcements:

• As you explore the following pages of puzzles and riddles, you'll come across all kinds of amazing sea creatures—birds in tuxedos, whales bigger than dinosaurs, and coral that looks like the human brain. If you're having trouble reeling in certain answers, feel free to fish around in the definitions for helpful clues and information. And it's okay to guess.

• The travel plan for this journey is up to you! You don't have to go in order from start to finish. Flip through the pages and stop wherever something strikes your fancy. If you're wild about penguins, you might jump in on page 87, which has some puzzlers about your favorite animal.

• For lunch, we recommend stopping for a Seafood Sampler at Carol's Clam Shack, on pages 4 and 5. See if you can guess the names of the ten scrumptious seafood dishes on the menu.

• As you roam through the ocean landscapes in this book, feel free to collect a few treasures for souvenirs—interesting facts about everything from shells to seaweeds to sharks.

And so, without further ado, grab your pencils and dive in. Bon voyage!

Underwater PICTURE PUZZLES

Double-Talk

Each of the sea creatures pictured on this page shares a name with another item shown below, although they are not always spelled the same way. See how many matches you can make by **drawing a line between each pair.**

Marine Menagerie

The four squares below are filled with all kinds of ocean animals. While each of the animals appears more than once, only three of them **can be found in all four squares.** Can you figure out which three they are?

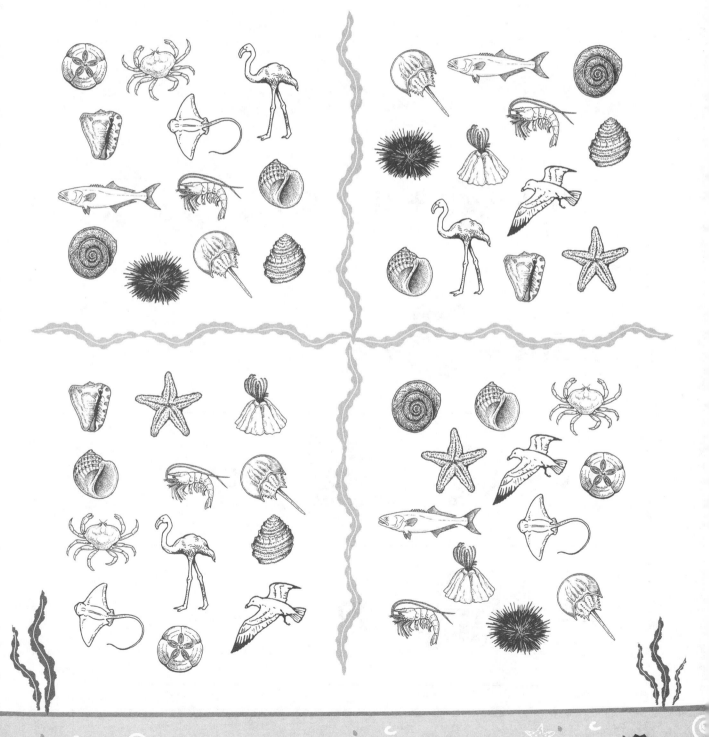

Seafood Sampler

There are **ten seafood specials on the menu** at Carol's Clam Shack. The only problem is that all the entrees are written in code. See how long it takes you to figure out what they are. Write your answers on the lines below each puzzle.

1. fr + 👁 + d   c + 🐑 🐑

_____

2. Sue + 🧑 + e

_____

3. c + 🐑 🐕 + der

_____

4. s + 🚗 + go

_____

5. br +  + d   s +  – r + + s

_____

6. &

_____

7. + ye +

_____

8.  + ers

_____

9. oi +   s + 2

_____

10. + rmp   scam +

_____

Telling Tails

Marine animals use their tails to propel themselves through the water. The shape of a tail can have a lot to do with how fast a creature can swim. Fish with crescent-shaped and forked tails are usually fast swimmers, while those with rounded or flat tails tend to move more slowly. Can you unscramble the letters below to **identify what sea creatures' tails are shown?**

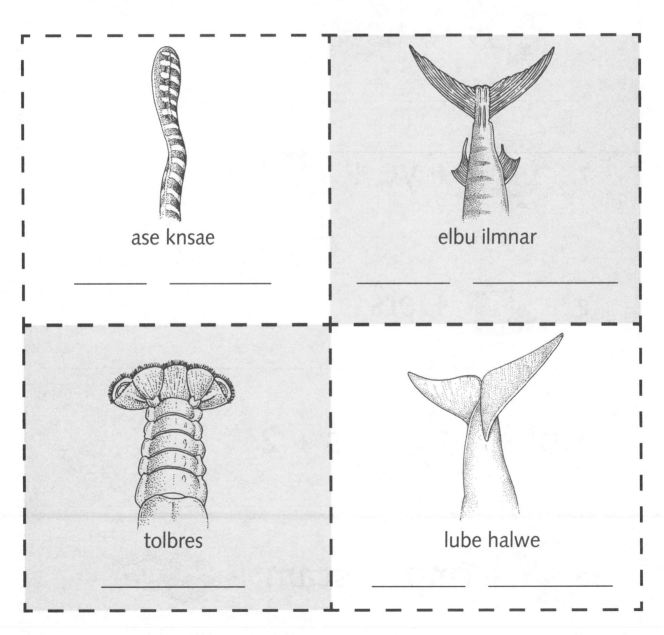

ase knsae

_____ _____

elbu ilmnar

_____ _____

tolbres

_____

lube halwe

_____ _____

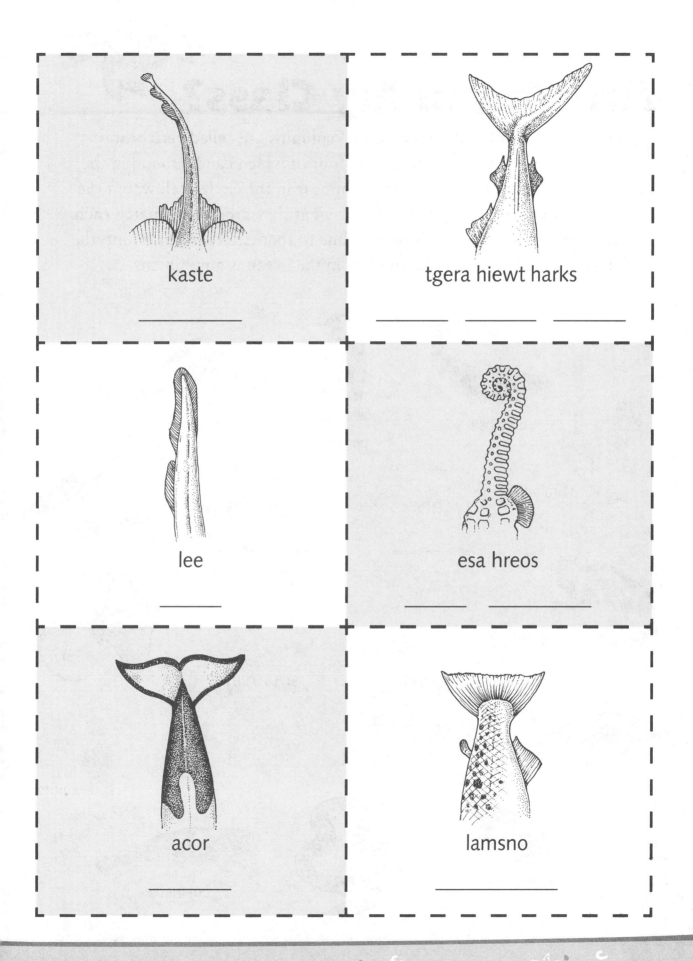

kaste

_____

tgera hiewt harks

_____ _____ _____

lee

_____

esa hreos

_____ _____

acor

_____

lamsno

_____

Are You In My Class?

Animals that have backbones or spinal columns are called vertebrates. There are five classes of vertebrates, four of which can be found in the ocean. The names of those four classes appear in the circles below, but the letters are scrambled. Can you figure out what they are? Then, match each animal to its proper class by drawing a line to that circle. Here's a hint: the one class of vertebrates that doesn't live in the ocean is amphibians.

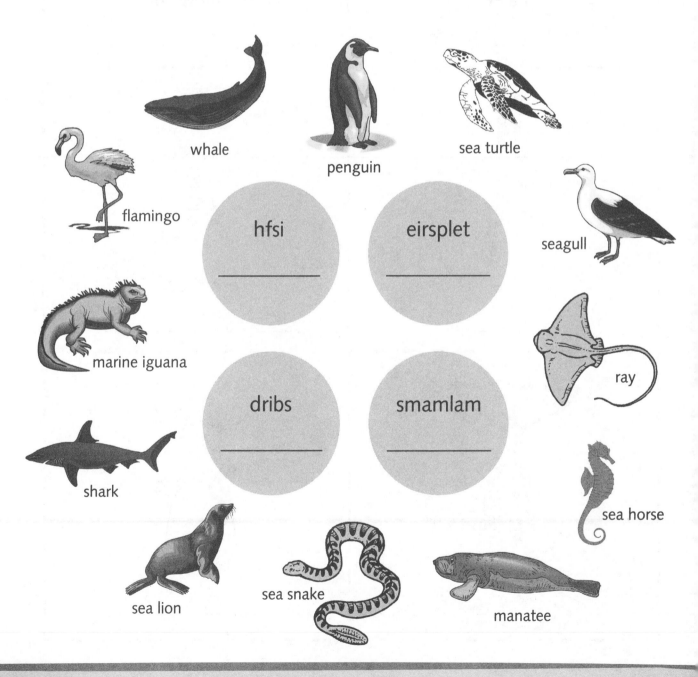

whale

penguin

sea turtle

flamingo

hfsi

_____

eirsplet

_____

seagull

marine iguana

dribs

_____

smamlam

_____

ray

shark

sea lion

sea snake

manatee

sea horse

Seaside Charades

These six clue boxes represent ocean-related words or expressions. To arrive at the answers, you'll need to **use your imagination** and consider all the parts that make up each picture.

1 _____

2 _____

3 _____

4 _____

I **love** being a clam!

5 _____

6 _____

Whale Words

There's plenty to say about whales. For starters, **whales are the biggest animals to have ever lived on earth.** That's one of the reasons they're so at home in the sea — the ocean waters help hold up their incredible tonnage. The images below stand for five words that are associated with this amazing marine mammal. Read the clues and see if you can figure out what they are.

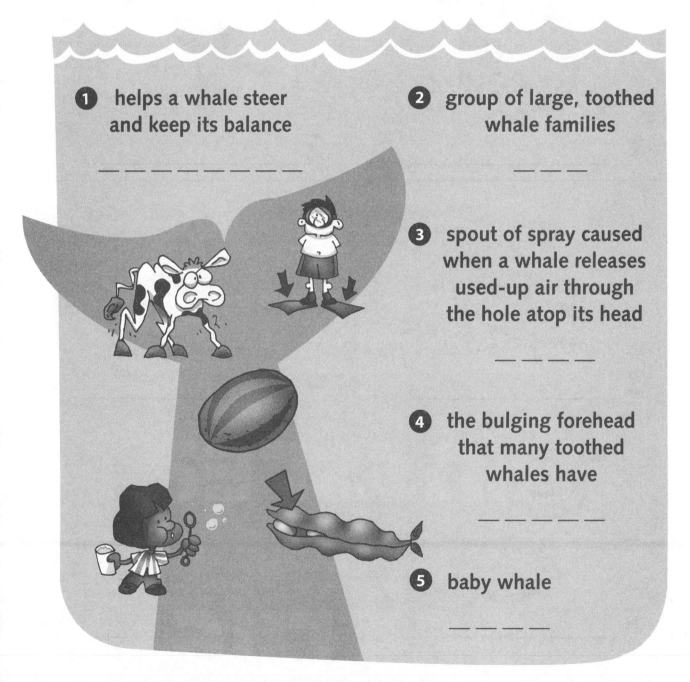

1 helps a whale steer and keep its balance

_ _ _ _ _ _ _ _ _

2 group of large, toothed whale families

_ _ _ _

3 spout of spray caused when a whale releases used-up air through the hole atop its head

_ _ _ _ _

4 the bulging forehead that many toothed whales have

_ _ _ _ _ _

5 baby whale

_ _ _ _ _

Creature Feature

This one is hard! Can you do it?

Many ocean and land animals have similar physical traits, such as markings or snouts. Check out the fish below, each of which has a two-part name. The first part matches the name of their look-alike animal. Match up the animals, then put the correct first name in the blank behind the fish. The dog snapper has been done for you.

_____ butterfly fish

_____ shark

*dog* snapper

_____ grouper

_____ fish

_____ lionfish

_____ ray

Spineless Sea Creatures

Below are clues to the names of twelve seafaring invertebrates. That means that **not one of them has a backbone.** Still, they all have other traits that equip them for life in the ocean. To make it easier to identify the animals, read the hints, then try your luck at solving the picture clues.

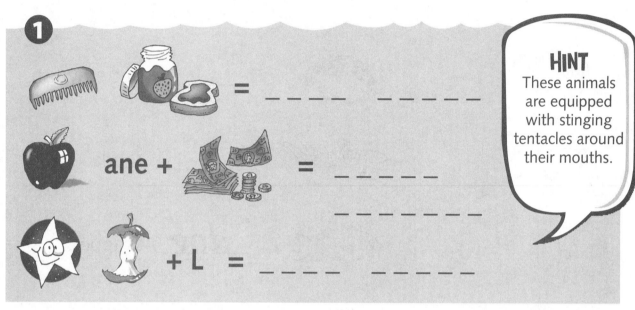

HINT
These animals are equipped with stinging tentacles around their mouths.

HINT
These creatures are radially symmetrical (shaped like a wheel) and have skeletons on the outsides of their bodies.

 **3**

 = _ _ _   _ _ _ _ _

HINT
These animals
have soft bodies.

B + 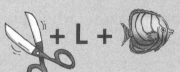 = _ _ _ _ _ _ _ _ _ _

_ _ _ _ _ _ _ _ _ _

 scal + ↑ = _ _ _ _ _ _ _ _ _ _ _

_ _ _ _ _ _ _

4

HINT
These critters have
bodies that are made
up of small parts
called segments.

 lob + = _ _ _ _ _ _ _ _

_ _ _ _ _ _ _ _

a +  + ac + L = _ _ _ _ _ _

_ _ _ _ _ _ _ _

 c + – bit = _ _ _ _ _ _ _ _ _ _ _

_ _ _ _

Bodybuilding

The sea creatures on these two pages are quite different from one another, but they have one thing in common. **They all have names that include body parts.** See how long it takes you to fill in the appropriate names. Hint: Count the blanks for each word to find out how many letters it has. One body part word will be used twice.

1 donkey's _ _ _ abalone

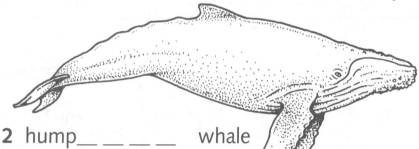

2 hump_ _ _ _ whale

3 four_ _ _ butterfly fish

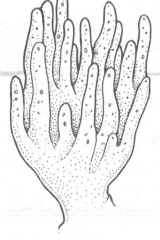

4 _ _ _ _ _ _ _ sponge

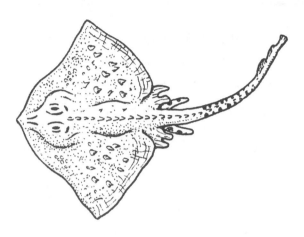

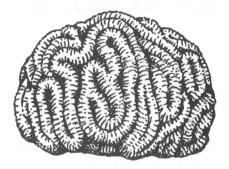

6 _ _ _ _ _ _ coral

5 thorn_ _ _ _ ray

8 logger_ _ _ _ turtle

7 spiny ur_ _ _ _

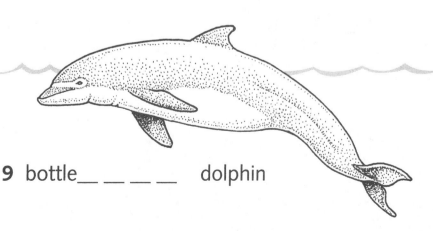

9 bottle_ _ _ _ dolphin

For answers see page 118

Coral Collection

Coral reefs may look like underwater trees and plants, but they're actually large colonies (clusters) of tiny animals called polyps. Unlike most vertebrates, a polyp's skeleton is located on the outside of its body. Layers and layers of these little skeletons make up a reef's stony structure. Below is a collection of picture clues that identify a bunch of different coral varieties.

1

_ _ _ _ _ _

2

+ Z

_ _ _ _

3

C +

_ _ _ _

4

L +

_ _ _ _ _ _ _

5

_ _ _ _ _ _ _ _

6

_ _ _ _

7

_ _ _ _ _ _ _ _ _ _ _ _

8

+ gan

_ _ _ _ _ _ _

9

B +

_ _ _ _ _

FATHOM THAT! Some coral reefs live for a hundred thousand years or more and grow to enormous sizes. The Great Barrier Reef off the coast of Australia is big enough to show up in pictures taken from outer space.

Underwater Picture Puzzles **17**

Food for Thought

Many sea animals are named after foods, because of their shape, color, or markings. Pictured below are 12 foods, and on the next page is a list of 12 animals with clues to their names. Think about how the bold words in each clue might describe one of the pictured foods.

CLUES

SEA CREATURES

1 Has a thin shell that **gets smaller at one end**
_____ whelk

2 Has a **smooth** shell that lets it easily plow through the sand
_____ snail

3 Is a member of the dolphin family and has a **roundish** head
_____-head whale

4 Can survive in **salty** places where other plants would not
_____weed

5 Has claws strong enough to crack open the **hard-shelled fruit** it likes to eat
_____ crab

6 Has a small **oval-shaped** shell
_____ stone clam

7 Is **distinctively** marked
_____ shrimp

8 Has a **ruffled** frill along its back
_____ sea slug

9 Forms a tight **fruit-shaped ball** when disturbed
_____anemone

10 Is a deep **yellow** color
_____ shark

11 Has **dark morsel-like** knobs in the center of its disk
_____ chip star

12 Has a **tube-shaped** body with a leathery outer skin
sea _____

Guess That Gastropod

The following picture puzzles represent nine members of the mollusk family. **Called gastropods, they have one-piece shells,** like snails and periwinkles. To guess their names, combine the letters and picture names that go with each shell. It helps to say the words out loud. Beside each shell is the correct number of blanks for the letters in each gastropod's name.

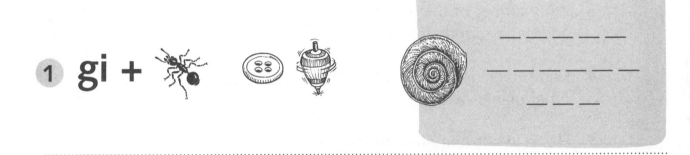

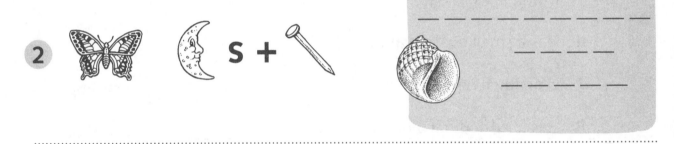

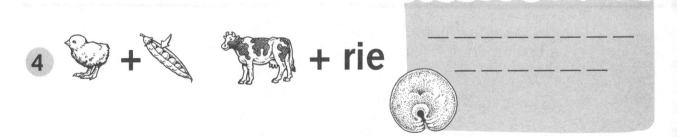

5. ＿ ＿ ＿ ＿ ＿ ＿
＿ ＿ ＿
＿ ＿ ＿

6. ＿ ＿ ＿ ＿ ＿
＿ ＿ ＿ ＿

7. ＿ ＿ ＿ ＿ ＿ ＿ ＿
＿ ＿ ＿ ＿

wh +

8. ＿ ＿ ＿ ＿
＿ ＿ ＿ ＿

9. ＿ ＿ ＿ ＿ ＿ ＿
＿ ＿ ＿ ＿ ＿ ＿

Sea Sounds

HINT! Trouble spelling an animal name? Guess the first letter, then look for it in Deep Sea Definitions.

Each of the pictures below stands for **the first syllable of a sea animal's name.** The incomplete names are listed on the right. Here's the tricky part: although the object or action may sound the same, it may not be spelled the same way. Make the right matches based on sound, and then print the correct letters in the spaces provided.

1 _ _ _ _ **g u i n**

2 _ _ _ _ **p h i n**

3 _ _ **g o n g**

4 _ _ _ _ **p o i s e**

5 _ _ _ _ _ **f i s h**

6 _ _ _ _ _ _ **r a y**

BONUS QUESTION
One of the answers to the puzzle on this page is an animal that's more closely related to the elephant than any other sea animal. Even though it can grow fairly large, it's still a graceful swimmer. In fact, early sailors sometimes mistook these creatures for mermaids. Do you know which animal it is?

What's the Word?

Below are picture clues for **words associated with different sea animals.** Can you match them with the definitions for each word? When you solve the clues, draw a line from each picture to the definition that goes with it.

s +

_ _ _ _ _ _

_ _ _ _ _

+ ers

_ _ _ _ _ _ _

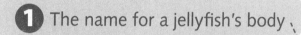
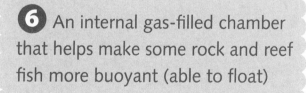

❶ The name for a jellyfish's body

❷ The mineral that coral polyps filter from the water to make their skeletons

❸ What a sea urchin uses to chisel out a home in solid rock

❹ The ink of a squid or cuttlefish shoots out from this body part

❺ What an otter uses to feel its way around underwater

❻ An internal gas-filled chamber that helps make some rock and reef fish more buoyant (able to float)

b e l l

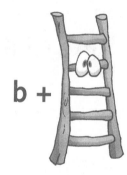

b +

_ _ _ _ _ _

+

_ _ _ _ _ _ _ _

Which Whale?

Many whales, including dolphins and porpoises, have **lots of teeth for hunting and eating fish and squid.** But most of the big whales have comb-like strainers called baleen to filter the tiny krill they feed on from the water. To solve this two-part puzzle, first fill in the name of the whale identified in each picture clue, and then draw a line from that box to the kind of whale you think it is: toothed or baleen.

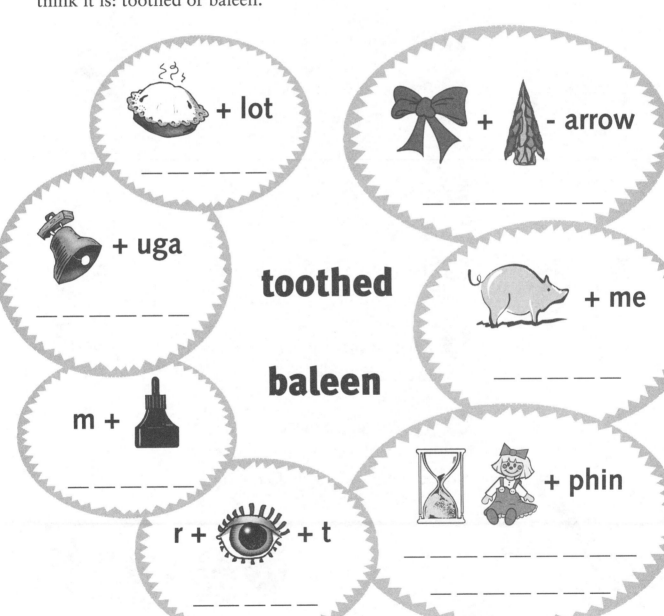

+ lot

_____

+ uga

_____

m +

_____

r + + t

_____

+ - arrow

_____

toothed

baleen

+ me

_____

+ phin

_____

_____

Marine FUN & GAMES

The Hungry Gulls

Every day the local fishermen leave some of the day's catch on the pier for the harbor seagulls. Assuming that the gulls will go for the biggest fish, which one will they swoop in on first? Circle your answer.

FATHOM THAT!
When a flounder first hatches, it resembles many other fish and lives near the surface of the water. Over time, one eye moves to the other side of the body and the flounder swims on its side along the ocean floor.

Prey Way

With suction cups on its arms, a hungry starfish has no problem opening up shellfish and pulling apart sea urchins. Of course, a sea star itself makes a tasty meal for other sea animals. The object of this puzzle is to **lead the starfish safely out of the maze.** You can pass right over any of its prey (oysters or urchins) but not its predators (crabs or seagulls).

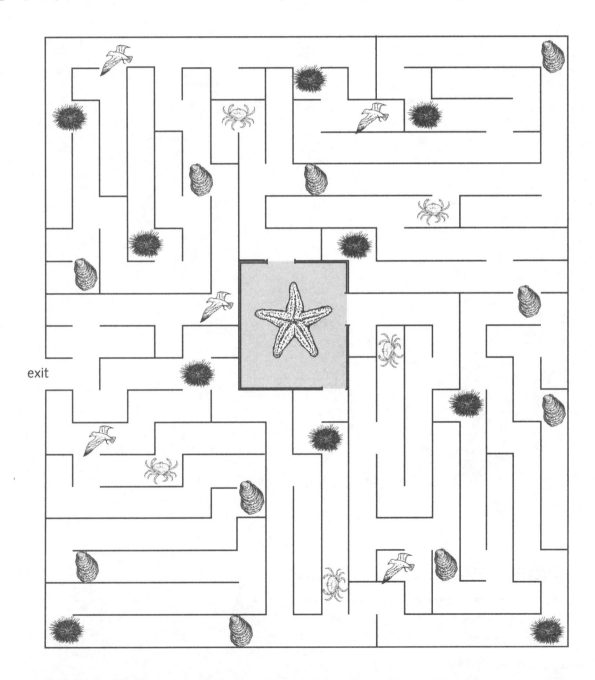

exit

Flip-Flop Fish

Things were going swimmingly for this little fish until he spotted the hungry harbor seal. Now he'll need to make a super quick turnaround to avoid disaster. Can you help him out by moving just four of the lines that make up his body (you can move his eye, too), so that he's heading back toward the surface?

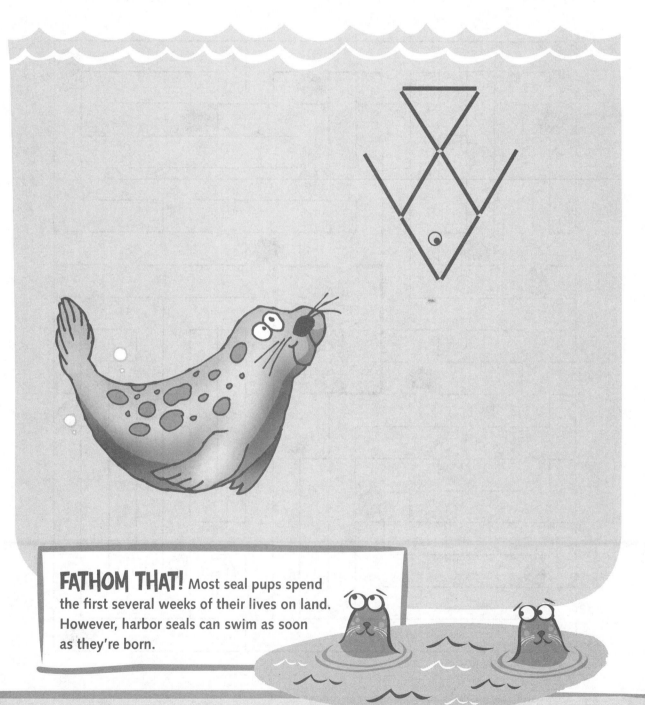

FATHOM THAT! Most seal pups spend the first several weeks of their lives on land. However, harbor seals can swim as soon as they're born.

See Birds

HINT! If you pull each symbol apart, you'll see that it is really a collection of letters.

Some birds are well-suited for life around or in the ocean. They have feathers that don't get wet, feet that are webbed for fast swimming, and beaks that are great for snatching fish. Even so, some have become extinct over time, one of which is represented below. Can you figure out which birds the following symbols stand for, and which one no longer exists? There's a hint printed upside down at the bottom of the page.

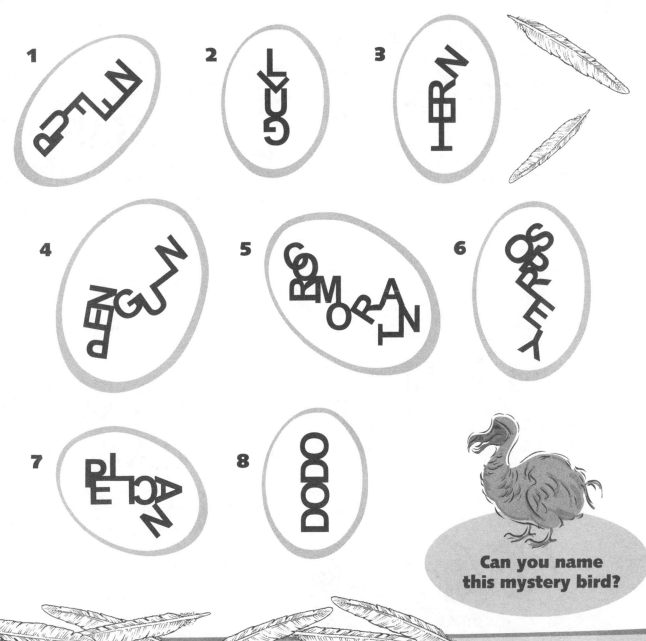

Can you name this mystery bird?

Auto Animals

The employees at Amazing Aquarium have special license plates on their cars, which represent their favorite sea animals. Sometimes the letters and numbers on the plates form a code for the creature's name. Sometimes they symbolize a distinguishing trait or habit. Can you figure out the animal each plate stands for? For example, LICNZ PL8 is code for LICENSE PLATE.

1

OCEAN STATE
SAM N
AMAZING AQUARIUM

2

OCEAN STATE
C STAR
AMAZING AQUARIUM

3

OCEAN STATE
IM N EL
AMAZING AQUARIUM

4

OCEAN STATE
2NA
AMAZING AQUARIUM

5

OCEAN STATE
SK8
AMAZING AQUARIUM

_____

6

OCEAN STATE
2 CLOZ
AMAZING AQUARIUM

_____

7

OCEAN STATE
MAN A T
AMAZING AQUARIUM

_____

8

OCEAN STATE
C NMNE
AMAZING AQUARIUM

_____

9

OCEAN STATE
8 RMZ
AMAZING AQUARIUM

10

OCEAN STATE
LFNT C L
AMAZING AQUARIUM

_____

Penguin Parade

There are 17 species of penguins in the world, and **each one has distinctive markings.** For example, all African penguins, like the ones below, have a particular black stripe on their chests. But each bird also has its very own pattern of black spots. Like human fingerprints, no two patterns of spots are the same. Take a look at the group of African penguins below and see how long it takes you to identify which individual is pictured twice.

Well Armed

It's nighttime and the **octopus has come out of his den.** Take a close look at the signs he is holding. Each symbol stands for something, but one of them is missing. If you can figure out what it is and look at the symbols together, left to right, you'll know what the octopus is hunting for. An extra hint is upside down at the bottom of the page.

FATHOM THAT! Giant Pacific octopi live along the rocky coast and in tide pools from Alaska to southern California. They are very talented creatures. When tested, they've been able to solve mazes and unscrew jar lids to get the food inside.

Hint: Each symbol is made from a letter of the alphabet.

Sardine School

For fish, **spending time in schools is a really smart thing to do.** No kidding! When a bigger, faster fish comes looking for lunch, it's harder to be singled out in a crowd. Here's a fun challenge that will put your division skills to the test. See if you can draw just three more lines like the one below to separate this school into seven groups, each containing a different number of fish. The only rule is that each line must connect two of the lifesaver rings.

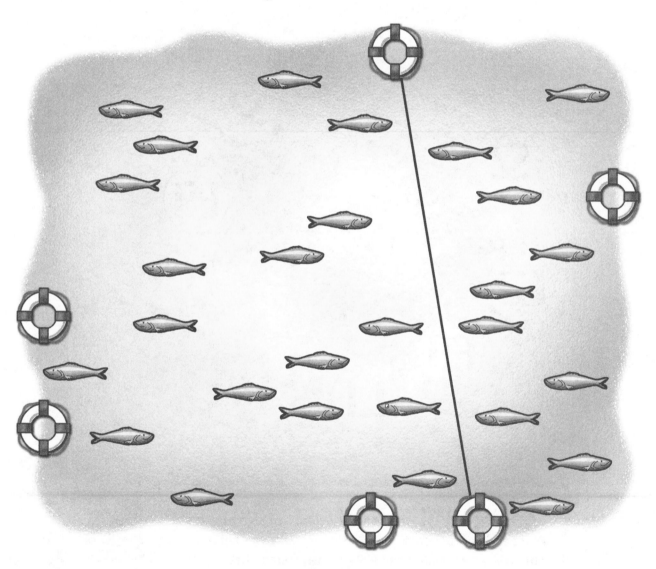

Crustacean Cubes

Pictured in the grid below are seven different crustaceans:

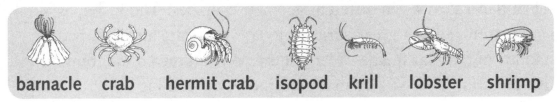

barnacle   crab   hermit crab   isopod   krill   lobster   shrimp

The challenge of this puzzle is to draw (or print the name of) one of those creatures in each of the empty boxes so that **no animal appears more than once per row or column.**

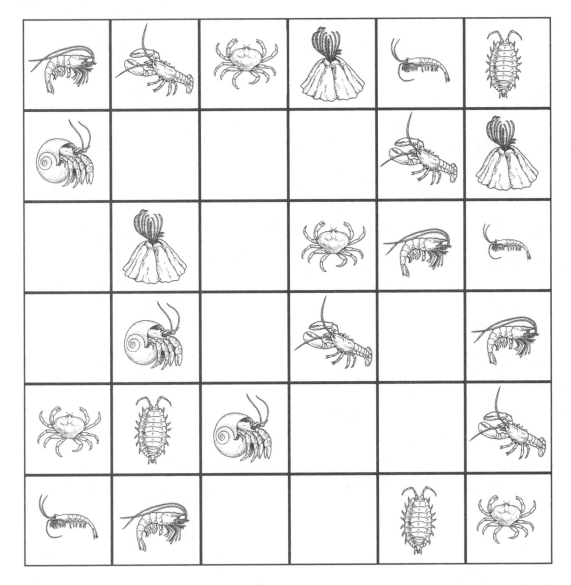

One Fish, Two Fish

Tangram puzzles, an ancient Chinese art, are made by cutting a square sheet of paper into seven different geometric shapes. Those shapes can then be arranged in a great variety of ways to create animals, people, and all kinds of familiar images. Here's how you can **turn a tangram into three fish pictures.** Once you've mastered those, try coming up with some of your own.

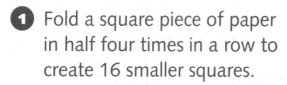

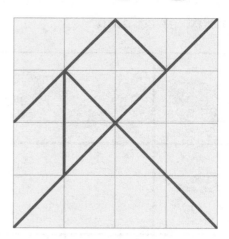

1 Fold a square piece of paper in half four times in a row to create 16 smaller squares.

2 Spread the paper flat, then draw cutting lines on the paper, as shown.

3 Cut along the lines to create these seven shapes. Then see if you can rearrange the pieces to create the images on the facing page. It takes all seven shapes to create each group of fish.

One Fish

Two Fish

Three Fish

Marine All-Stars

Not only are there plenty of fish in the sea, there are quite a few celebrities, too. Listed below are **some pretty famous nautical characters.** See if you can match their names with the types of sea animals they are.

Flipper	*sea turtle*
Charlie	*crab*
Jaws	*clown fish*
Nemo	*tuna*
Patrick	*penguin*
Sebastian	*sperm whale*
Willy	*starfish*
Chilly Willy	*dolphin*
Moby Dick	*killer whale*
Crush	*great white shark*

FATHOM THAT! The decorator crab has a fascinating way of disguising itself to hide from predators. It adorns its shell with algae, sea sponges, and sea anemones.

The Diving Otter

To keep warm, a sea otter relies on its extra dense fur (it doesn't have blubber like seals do) and eats as much as 20 pounds of food a day. It can dive as deep as 180 feet to search out clams and other shellfish. **Find the round-trip route** the otter will take to pick up the clam on the ocean floor and bring it back up to the surface. Travel on any portion of the maze just once; retracing or crossing over your path is not allowed.

Catch the Drift

All of the puzzles shown here represent phrases or expressions that relate to ocean life or the sea itself. To solve them you need to think beyond the specific words or letters and think about the way they are presented within the box.

7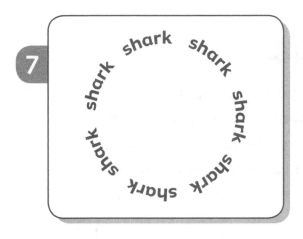

8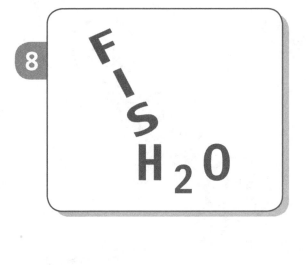

9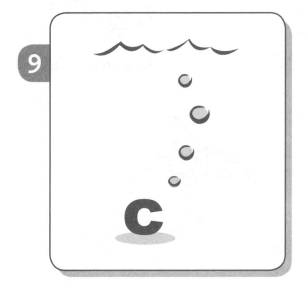

10

11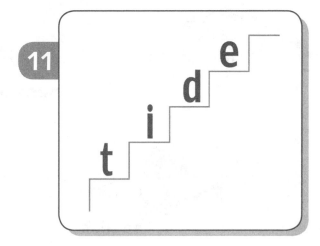

12

Swift Swimmers

Most of the time, the fastest ocean animals cruise along at a comfortable 5 to 10 miles per hour. But for short distances, some sea creatures can really turn on the juice, reaching speeds of over 60 miles per hour. **If the animals shown here were racing each other** in a swim meet, how do you think they would do? Draw a line from each one to the place where you think it would finish.

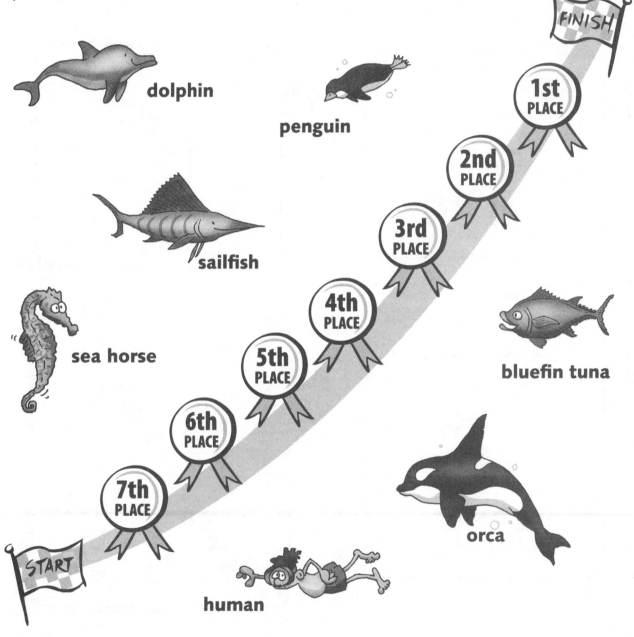

dolphin

penguin

sailfish

sea horse

bluefin tuna

orca

human

For answers see page 126

Ocean WORD PUZZLES

Tidepool Tally

The sandy and rocky saltwater tidepools that form all along the seacoast are home to an amazing range of interesting creatures. Hidden in this puzzle are 12 tidepool dwellers, listed below. The letters of their names are always in a straight line, but may be printed across, up and down, diagonally, forward, or backward. So, just like the real animals themselves, they can be tricky to spot — but if you keep at it you're bound to discover them all.

```
P  L  E  K  S  P  O  N  G  E
F  E  N  O  M  E  N  A  B  H
C  U  R  C  H  I  N  V  K  S
G  R  L  I  A  N  S  Z  M  I
H  W  A  S  W  P  Y  L  U  F
A  C  U  B  H  I  S  E  S  R
L  I  M  P  E  T  N  F  S  A
G  P  G  B  L  A  H  K  E  T
A  N  J  D  K  X  R  I  L  S
E  L  C  A  N  R  A  B  K  E
```

algae	kelp	periwinkle	starfish
anemone	limpet	snail	urchin
barnacle	mussel	sponge	whelk
crab			

Deep-Sea Circles

Even in the deep, deep sea where no sunlight reaches, ocean life exists — although the creatures that are at home there have traits that make them rather unusual! If you pick the right place to start on each circle and read the letters clockwise in some cases, counterclockwise in others, they will spell out the name of the particular deep-sea fish described in the center.

This fish has a long, tapering tail that looks like a rodent.

T T A A I L R L R

This fierce fish has needle-sharp teeth and makes a hissing sound.

V R E P I V

Using its long fins like fishing rods, this small fish lures smaller fish toward its mouth.

E R A L N G

This fish is shaped like a chopping tool and has organs that light up along its stomach and tail.

H C T E A A T H

Better Letters

Hidden in the single words and word pairs below are a total of 20 different sea animals. To round them up, all you need to do is **change one letter per word.**

1 snarl _ _ _ _ _

2 mobster _ _ _ _ _ _ _

3 drill _ _ _ _ _ _

4 other _ _ _ _ _

5 scrimp _ _ _ _ _ _

6 slam _ _ _ _

7 pod _ _ _

8 hull _ _ _ _

9 sass _ _ _ _ _

10 deal _ _ _ _

11 see belly _ _ _ _ _ _ _ _

12 land collar _ _ _ _ _ _ _ _ _ _

13 purse sharp _ _ _ _ _ _ _ _ _ _ _

14 moral eek _ _ _ _ _ _ _ _

15 clue drab _ _ _ _ _ _ _ _

16 set plug _ _ _ _ _ _ _

17 tea pan _ _ _ _ _ _

18 tiller shale _ _ _ _ _ _ _ _ _ _

19 pea loon _ _ _ _ _ _ _

20 set stir _ _ _ _ _ _ _

Name It

If you insert the ten human names shown here into the appropriate blanks below, you'll end up with a list of **ten different sea creatures.**

ROSE
ELLY
DOTTY
ANGEL
VALLY
RAY
HAL
ANN
MARLIN
MACK

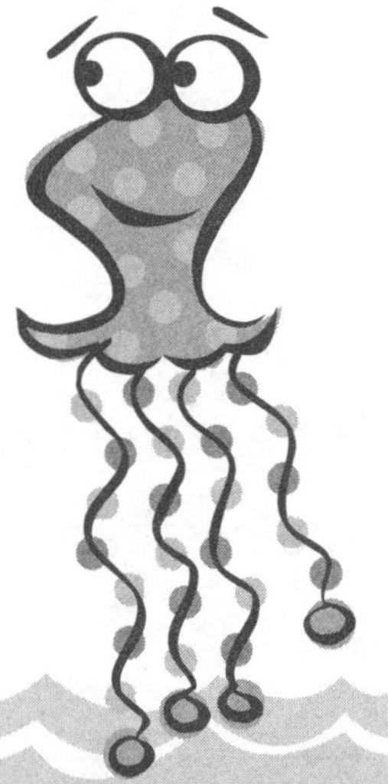

1 ____________ IBUT

2 STING ____________

3 B ____________ ERFISH

4 ________________ CORAL

5 J ________________ FISH

6 ________________ EREL

7 TRE ____________________

8 ____________________ BACK

9 ____________________ SHARK

10 BLUE ________________________

For answers see page 127

Who's Who Clues

Here's a puzzle that makes a **game** of coming up with animal **names**. Just think of a word that completes each **rhyme**, and you'll have all the answers in almost no **time**.

1 They call me a dogfish
but you won't hear me bark.
Though I'm smaller than others,
I'm still a true

_____

2 Wherever I go
I leave my trail.
With the shell on
my back,
I'm a marine

_____

3 If there's one thing for sure
of which I'm not keen,
it's crowded tin cans,
'cause I'm a

_____

4 How do I stay warm?
Here's the deal:
With my layer of blubber,
since I am a

_____

5 I'm playful and friendly.
I can stand on my tail.
You call me a dolphin,
and I'm a small

_____

6 I rely on my whiskers to
feel my way underwater.
Beware snails and clams,
'cause I'm one hungry

_____

7 When I spotted the penguin,
here's what I did:
I shot out black ink,
like any smart

_____

8 If a humpback finds me
he'll eat his fill.
I'm a tiny creature
known as

_____

Shark Scramble

Equipped with sharp senses, streamlined bodies, plenty of teeth, and bigger brains than most fish, sharks are one of the top predators in the sea. There are more than 400 species! The scrambled letters listed here represent a dozen types of sharks you may have heard of before. Can you figure out what they are?

1 tregi _____

2 koam _____

3 lube _____

4 awleh _____

5 kingsab _____

6 sreun _____

7 meemdahrah _____

8 melon _____

9 aertg ewith _____

10 darepol _____

11 randbas _____

12 baglerope _____

FATHOM THAT! Some sharks are hatched from eggs, as are skates, a relative of the shark. Their empty egg cases, which often wash ashore, are called mermaids' purses. Look for one like this drawing the next time you're at the beach.

Sea What I Mean

If you unscramble the letters on top of each grid correctly, you'll end up with **five familiar ocean-related phrases**. Once you've figured them out, transfer the letter from each number box to the row of boxes below and you'll spell out another fun sea saying.

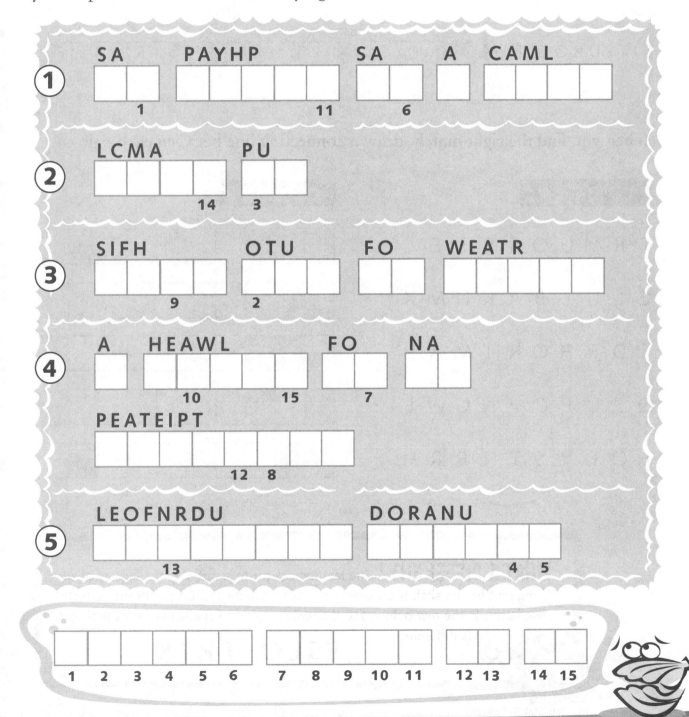

1. SA   PAYHP   SA   A   CAML
   (boxes with numbers 1, 11, 6)

2. LCMA   PU
   (boxes with numbers 14, 3)

3. SIFH   OTU   FO   WEATR
   (boxes with numbers 9, 2)

4. A   HEAWL   FO   NA
   (boxes with numbers 10, 15, 7)
   PEATEIPT
   (boxes with numbers 12, 8)

5. LEOFNRDU   DORANU
   (boxes with numbers 13, 4, 5)

Bottom row boxes: 1 2 3 4 5 6   7 8 9 10 11   12 13   14 15

Loggerhead Lunch

Slide each row of letters in Column A into the correct grid in Column B, and the letters in the unshaded boxes will spell out something that loggerhead turtles like to eat. For example: When the letters below are moved into the grid, the word **TURTLE** comes clearly into view.

B I T S U R O T L E → ☐☐☐☐☐☐☐☐☐☐ = ☐☐ T ☐ U R ☐ T L E

When you find the right match, draw a connecting line between each pair.

T R M U O S P S E L

C L U L B A K N M X

S D S H O R I M A P

Q S U P O V N G W E

F O E Y S T I E R H

WHAT'S DIFFERENT? The leatherback turtle is not only the largest of all living reptiles, its shell is different from other sea turtles. Cross out the correct five letters in the row below, and the remaining word spells out how the shell is different.

E S L O P F R T K

Team Up

Sometimes **the name you call an animal** depends on how old it is or how many of them there are. In the center column, you'll find the common name of eight adult sea creatures. Try matching each one to its correct baby name (left column) and group name (right column).

> **HEY!** Some of these words are hard! It helps to check Deep Sea Definitions!

BABY	COMMON NAME	GROUP
fry	FISH	pod
pup	EEL	smack
spat	JELLYFISH	rookery
elver	OTTER	school
ephyna	OYSTER	bed
calf	PENGUIN	swarm
chick	WHALE	raft

Wacky Rhyme Time

The following words are clues to funny rhyming phrases, each of which features a different sea animal. Here's an example to get you under way: Suppose the clue words were **leatherback jump**. A leatherback is a type of turtle, and a jump could also be called a hurdle. Put the two together and you get **turtle hurdle**.

1 moray tire

2 cod plate

3 mollusk preserves

4 gastropod path

5 sea mammal supper

6 boring seabird

STUMPED? You'll find clues for mollusk, gastropod, and cephalaopod in Deep Sea Definitions.

7 magnificent ray

8 cephalopod cover

9 orca story

10 hammerhead boat

11 moonlight albacore

12 sea cow tent

FATHOM THAT! When a hungry moon snail finds a clam, it surrounds the shell with its big foot. Then it uses a file-like tongue to drill through the shell to the clam's soft insides.

For answers see page 128

Fish Find

Believe it or not, sixteen different kinds of fish are swimming around in the box below. Their names may be spelled forward, backward, up, down, or diagonally—but always in a straight line. When you've netted the very last one, transfer the unused letters into the row of boxes below. This bonus answer tells you where in the sea you can find lots of fish.

```
G  G  N  I  R  R  E  H  R
O  Y  S  A  S  N  L  E  E
A  B  Y  N  I  C  D  H  S
T  O  C  D  A  N  U  T  S
F  G  R  O  U  P  E  R  A
I  A  O  O  D  O  P  L  R
S  A  L  M  O  N  S  E  W
H  F  R  E  F  F  U  P  R
B  A  S  S  T  N  U  R  G
```

BONUS ANSWER

Hint: Look for these fish!

bass	puffer
eel	ray
flounder	salmon
sardine	boatfish
snapper	goby
grouper	tuna
grunt	wrasse
	herring

It's a Fact

Hidden in this puzzle is an interesting fact about fish. To spell it out, you need to start on a certain letter, then go around the triangle twice in the correct direction (to the left or to the right), stopping on every other letter. If you're feeling stuck, check out the upside-down clue at the bottom of the page.

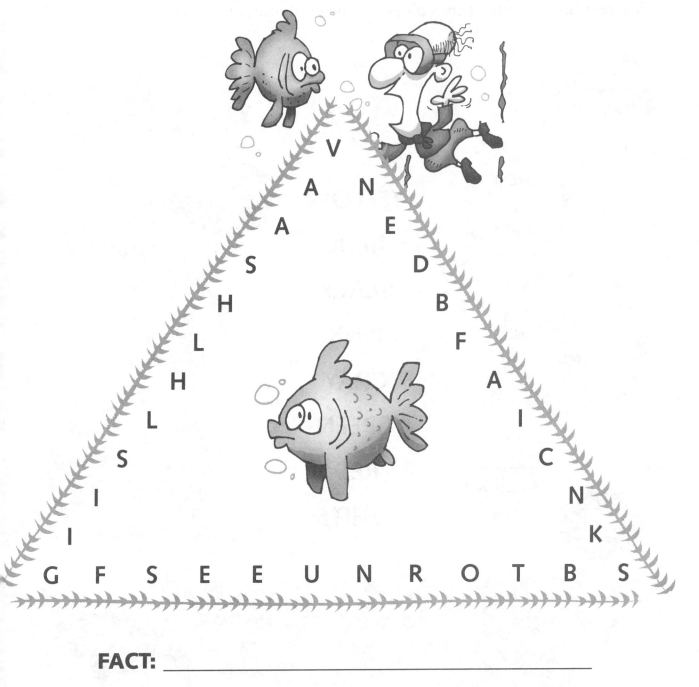

FACT: _____

Clue: The interesting fact starts with the letter "T".

Hue Are You?

Each of the bubbles on this page contains an incomplete name of an animal that lives in the sea. To solve the puzzle, draw a line connecting each bubble to the specific color that is meant to fill in the blank. Two of the names can be correctly completed with two or more different hues. Many of the colors will be used more than once.

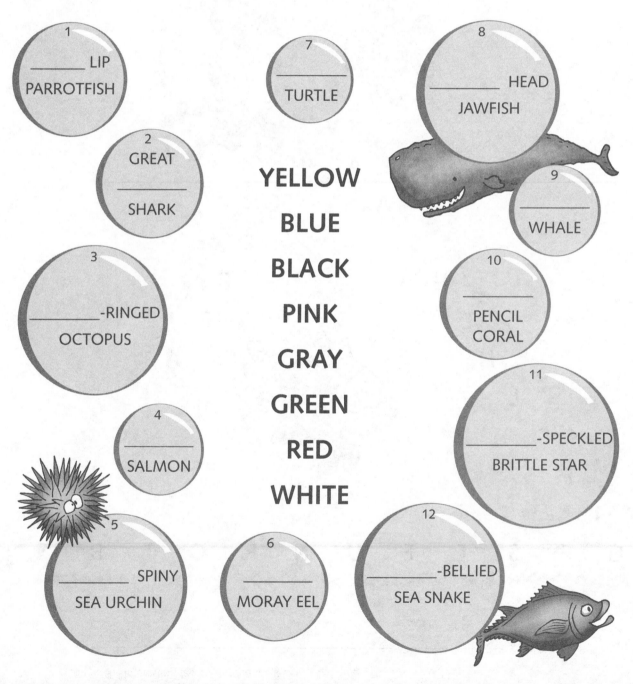

1
_____ LIP
PARROTFISH

7
_____
TURTLE

8
_____ HEAD
JAWFISH

2
GREAT
_____
SHARK

YELLOW

BLUE

BLACK

PINK

GRAY

GREEN

RED

WHITE

9
_____
WHALE

3
_____-RINGED
OCTOPUS

10
_____
PENCIL
CORAL

4
_____
SALMON

11
_____-SPECKLED
BRITTLE STAR

5
_____ SPINY
SEA URCHIN

6
_____
MORAY EEL

12
_____-BELLIED
SEA SNAKE

Sea Jelly Jazz

Jellyfish are equipped with **tentacles and stingers,** but they are missing a lot of other body parts. Identify six of them by connecting the letters that spell out the missing trait. You can go in any direction from any letter. In the end, all of the letters should be drawn through at least once. The first word, BLOOD, is done for you.

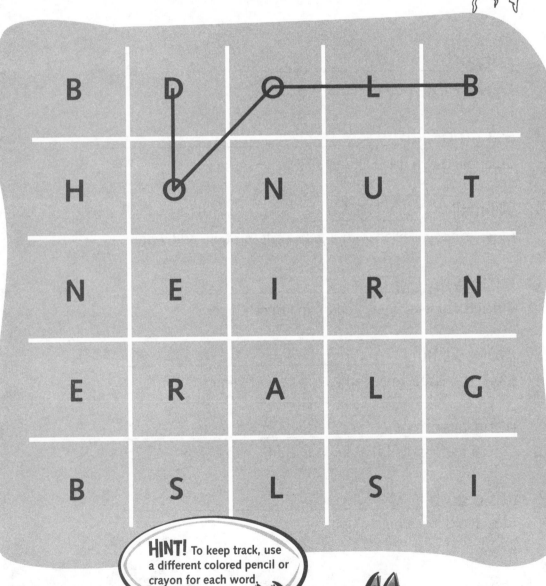

HINT! To keep track, use a different colored pencil or crayon for each word.

That Stings!

Many sea animals sting their prey. Seven are named below, but their names are scrambled. Use the clues to sort out each name and write it in the blank. Then find where the word fits in the boxes on the next page, and write it again. When you're done, the middle column of letters will spell out what the stingers are.

1   grityans _____

Clue: a relative of the shark

2   esa nmoeean _____   _____

Clue: the clown fish is unaffected by its poison

3   yelhifslj _____

Clue: its body is filled with a gel of salt, protein, and water

4   eas paws _____   _____

Clue: its name reminds you of an insect stinger

5   pronocis hifs _____   _____

Clue: its fins are equipped with a sack of venom

6   ribna craol _____   _____

Clue: a reef resident that looks like a human organ

7   aes cruinh _____   _____

Clue: looks like a pincushion

FATHOM THAT!
The Portuguese man-of-war looks like a jellyfish, but it isn't one. It's actually a colony of hundreds of polyps hanging from a gas-filled floating bubble — and it's capable of delivering a very powerful sting!

Ocean Word Puzzles   **61**

Shuffle Squares

The hammerhead shark is truly a fascinating creature. It has **a mallet-shaped head,** which it uses to pin down its prey. The answer to this puzzle will tell you another fact about hammerheads. The nine letters inside each Block are correct, so don't change those. Change the order of the six Blocks to spell out a statement. The shaded blocks are spacers between the words.

Block 1	Block 2	Block 3	Block 4	Block 5	Block 6

Row 1: A R · A Y S E · W S T I · H A T N G R
Row 2: D S H E A · H A R H A M · K S · M E R
Row 3: A T · O E B E S · L I K T · E T

Block __	Block __	Block __	Block __	Block __	Block __

Salty City

You've just been hired at the Salty City post office to deliver mail. The first thing you notice is that the mail has only names but no addresses. That's because everybody in town lives on streets that are named after them. Here's today's batch of mail. See if you can match each name to the right address.

Ray Razor Clam	Seabird Square
Bobby Bottlenose	Crustacean Court
Linda Loggerhead	Whale Way
Michael Monk Seal	Dolphin Drive
Penelope Puffin	Pinniped Place
Oscar Orca	Fish Freeway
Krista Krill	Bivalve Boulevard
Sandra Snapper	Turtle Turnpike

HERE'S A CLUE!
Look up crustacean, pinniped, and bivalve in Deep Sea Definitions.

Sea-ing Double

The ten marine animals featured in this puzzle have something in common. Each of their names has a certain letter that appears twice in a row. In each row of boxes below, those two letters are in the right place. The remaining letters of each name are scrambled. See how long it takes you to put each letter where it belongs.

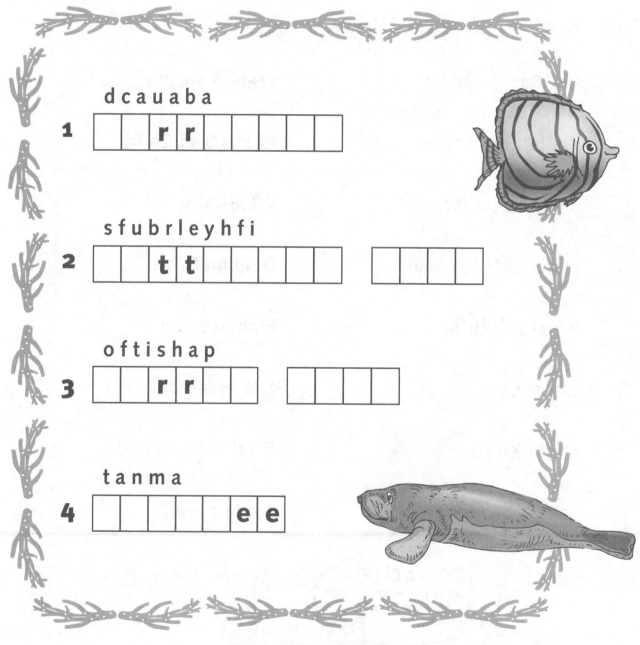

d c a u a b a

1 | | | r | r | | | | |

s f u b r l e y h f i

2 | | | t | t | | | | | | | |

o f t i s h a p

3 | | | r | r | | | | | |

t a n m a

4 | | | | | e | e |

Hint: Some of the animal answers are pictured on these two pages.

ribrealst

5 | | | | t | t | | | | | | | |

yihejsf

6 | | | l | l | | | | |

asdnodra

7 | | | | | | | | l | l | |

roe

8 | t | t | | |

bifracrel

9 | | | d | d | | | | | | | |

rtolardeheletu

10 | | | g | g | | | | | | | | | | | |

What Do You Call a Fish?

Listed below are some of the ways **people around the world** say the word FISH. Try matching each word to the correct language.

pez   Italian

poisson   Japanese

pesces   German

sakana   Spanish

fisch   French

Bonjour!

Distant Shores

The scrambled letters in front of each sea creature below represent a specific nationality (such as German or French) or country that is the first part of the animal's name. See if you can figure them out.

1. USEGROPTUE   _ _ _ _ _ _ _ _ _ _ _   MAN-O-WAR

2. NERCHF   _ _ _ _ _ _ _   GRUNT

3. NIXCAME   _ _ _ _ _ _ _   HOGFISH

4. SALKANA   _ _ _ _ _ _ _   KING CRAB

5. MANICRAE   _ _ _ _ _ _ _ _   EEL

6. WIGREANON   _ _ _ _ _ _ _ _ _   LOBSTER

7. FARICNA   _ _ _ _ _ _ _   PENGUIN

8. ANCHI   _ _ _ _ _   MOON SNAIL

Clam Up

There are plenty of ways to **cook up clams** for a seafood feast. The answers in this puzzle are five popular methods. As you solve the clues from the bottom up, each answer will provide an extra hint to the next one. Just copy the letter below the arrow into the block directly above it.

1 **First Clue:** Topped with bread crumbs and bacon.
Second Clue: It's also the name of a place where people go to play poker.

2 **First Clue:** Chopped up and cooked fritter style.
Second Clue: The second word of this food's name rhymes with "bakes."

3 **First Clue:** Cooked in a creamy broth.
Second Clue: Corn is another variety of this soup or stew.

4 **First Clue:** Battered and cooked in hot oil.
Second Clue: Chicken is sometimes cooked this way, too.

5 **First Clue:** Simmered and dipped in melted butter.
Second Clue: It's also a name given to ships powered by hot water vapor.

| M |

| C | L | A | M |

WANT A HINT?
Start at the bottom and work your way to the top!

For answers see page 132

You're Hired!

Imagine that **it's your job to round up a big crew** to put on an undersea extravaganza. You need carpenters to build the set, a cast of characters to perform a fairy-tale play, circus performers, and musicians. To sort it all out, all you need to do is use the clues provided in each category to identify the best ocean animals for the jobs. Good luck!

The Carpentry Crew

Hint: Think of tools and materials you use to build things.

__ __ __ __ __ __ **head shark** *has eyes are that wide apart*

__ __ __ **fish** *slashes schools of fish with its toothed snout*

__ __ __ __ __ __ **ton** *is made up of tiny plants and animals*

__ __ __ __ __ __ __ __ **fish** *has a blade-shaped, silvery body*

The Fairy-Tale Characters

Hint: Think of people in distress and scary creatures.

__ __ __ __ __ __ **fish** *is related to the clown fish*

sea __ __ __ __ __ __ __ *has a frilly body that looks like seaweed*

__ __ __ __ **eel** *has sharp teeth and lives in a rocky den*

The Circus Performers

Hint: Think of funny people and four-legged animals.

_ _ _ _ _ _ **fish** *has distinct markings and bobs when it swims*

_ _ _ _ _ _ **fish** *has a "mane" of hollow, poisonous spines*

_ _ _ _ _ _ _ _ _ **seal** *is the largest of its species*

sea _ _ _ _ _ _ *swims upright unlike other fish*

The Group of Musicians

Hint: Think of instruments with keys and strings.

_ _ _ _ _ _ _ _ _ _ **coral** *looks like a bunch of tubes*

_ _ _ _ _ _ _ _ **crab** *waves its large claws back and forth*

_ _ _ _ _ _ **fish** *is a skate with a body shaped like an instrument*

_ _ _ _ **seal** *has a horseshoe-shaped pattern on its back*

FATHOM THAT! Grunt fish have teeth deep in their throats. Sometimes they grind those teeth together, making a groaning noise — the very sound that earned them their name.

In a Word

If you combine all of the letters in each of the word pairs here and then rearrange them, you can **spell a sea creature's name.** To help you get started, two letters have already been put in the proper place on each line for you.

1   tea name   _ a _ _ t _ _ _

2   hold pin   _ _ l _ h _ _

3   ear shoes   _ e _   _ _ _ _ s _

4   cot soup   _ c _ o _ _ _

5   can pile   p _ _ _ _ _ _ n

6   his fails   _ _ i _ f _ _ _

7   black heater   _ _ _ t _ _ r _ _ _ _

8   wolf chins   _ _ _ w _ _ _ s _

9   round elf   _ l _ _ _ d _ _

10 any grits   _ _ _ _ g _ _ y

Feeding Frenzy

In each of these circles is one sea animal that is **eaten by all the other creatures** in it. Can you figure out which ones?

octopus
cuttlefish
loggerhead turtle
fish
shrimp
flamingo **squid**

clam **people**
eel
otter
sea star
whelk
seagull
flounder

seabirds krill
penguin
squid
seal
fish
whale

seagull
crab whelk
sea star
conch
worm
snail **oyster**

For answers see page 135

Can You Stomach It?

Over the years some surprising items have turned up in **sharks' stomachs.** The answers to this crossword identify 16 of them.

ACROSS

2   Metal cover on a car tire

4   Hooks, lures, and bobbins

7   Numbered tag on a car

9   Kitty is a _____

10 What a skeleton is made of

11 A marker that floats on water

13 It goes under the shingles on a roof

15 An animal similar to an alligator

16 This wakes you up in the morning

DOWN

1   What band members play

3   Worn on a foot

5   Wheel on a semi or pickup

6   What you wear

8   Piece of jewelry

12 Has two tires and handlebars

14 Tops a reindeer's head

Four of a Kind

As you probably know, there isn't just one kind of whale. There are many types, in many sizes, with different names. This is true of many sea animals. Below are the scrambled names of ten sea animals, with four of their types as clues. See how many of the solutions you can unscramble.

1 **BOSTLER** __ __ __ __ __ __ __
red, banded, armored, velvet

2 **RABC** __ __ __ __
fiddler, arrow, decorator, king

3 **CLOAR** __ __ __ __ __
carnation, pillar, fire, cactus

4 **KARSH** __ __ __ __ __
cookie cutter, lemon, cow, goblin

5 **NURCIH** __ __ __ __ __ __
cake, reef, heart, pencil

6 **MALNSO** __ __ __ __ __ __
sockeye, pink, chum, coho

7 **PRIMHS** __ __ __ __ __ __
barber pole, peppermint, sponge, snapping

8 **SALE** __ __ __ __
leopard, bearded, crabeater, ribbon

9 **AWELH** __ __ __ __ __
fin, minke, narwhal, pilot

10 **GUPNEIN** __ __ __ __ __ __ __
macaroni, rockhopper, emperor, chinstrap

Seaweed for Lunch?

You don't have to go to the beach to find seaweed. There's probably some in your kitchen right now! Seaweed is often used in food products to make them smooth and creamy. Fifteen of these products are hidden in this word puzzle. Once you've found them all, copy the unused letters, in order, in the spaces below to spell out a fun fact.

T	H	M	I	L	K	S	H	A	K	E
E	Y	L	L	E	J	Y	H	A	T	V
Y	E	S	A	U	C	E	T	S	C	Y
V	H	S	I	L	E	R	A	O	H	D
A	R	E	E	B	U	P	N	U	E	N
R	O	L	E	G	H	A	V	P	E	A
G	E	J	O	T	S	O	R	R	S	C
M	A	Y	O	N	N	A	I	S	E	O
M	O	O	P	U	D	D	I	N	G	T
S	T	E	N	I	R	A	G	R	A	M

Fact: _ _ _ _ _ _ _ _ _

_ _ _ _ _ _ _ _

_ _ _ _ _ _ _ .

Items to search for: beer, candy, cheese, gravy, jam, jelly, margarine, mayonnaise, milkshake, pudding, relish, sauce, soup, toothpaste, yogurt

Undersea Sculptures

You've probably heard of hot springs or geysers, such as Old Faithful. Similar springs, known as hydrothermal vents, occur on the ocean floor, where water seeps down to the earth's hot inner layers. There the water gets super-hot and blasts back up to the sea floor. A mixture of minerals comes up with the steam and eventually settles back down around the vents, forming chimneylike stacks called **black smokers**. Follow the clues below to guess the names scientists have given to some of them.

ACROSS

3 **First word:** what you call something you can't find
Second word: Phoenix, New York, Dayton (any one of these)

4 **One word:** home for insects that make honey

5 **One word:** a famous, giant lizard movie star

7 **First word:** very fortunate
Second word: three of these and you're out

8 **First word:** slithery reptile
Second word: what's in the middle of a peach

DOWN

1 **First word:** what you call something that doesn't work
Second word: metal object that fits onto a cowboy boot

2 **First word:** soot-filled air that rises from a fire
Second word: a common connecting word
Third word: glasses you can see yourself in

6 **First word:** a flower with thorns
Second word: a place to grow vegetables

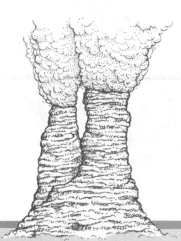

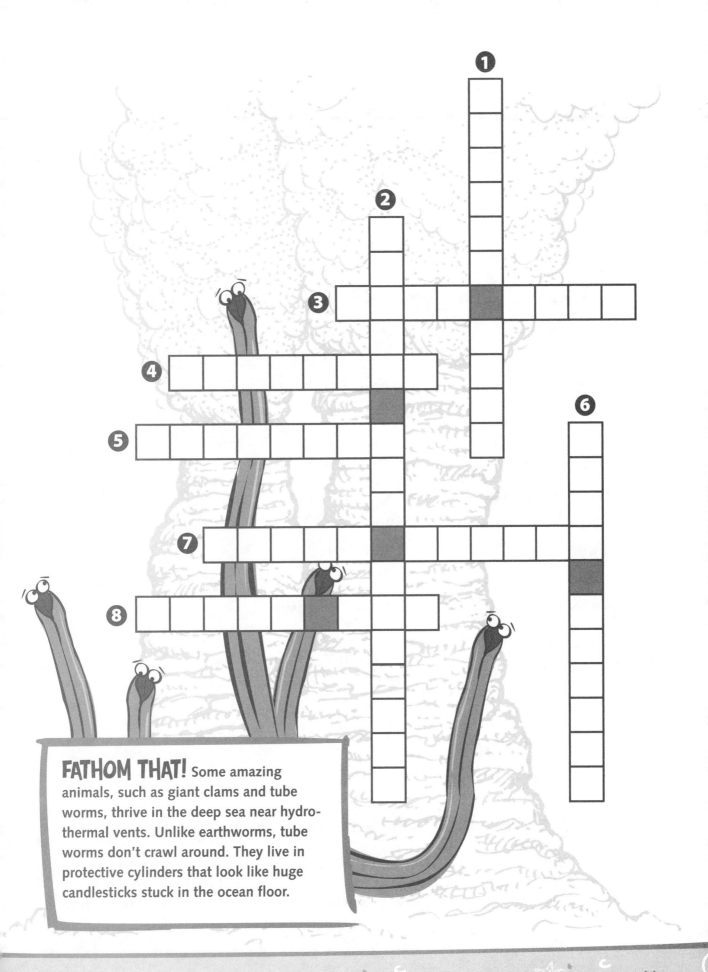

FATHOM THAT! Some amazing animals, such as giant clams and tube worms, thrive in the deep sea near hydrothermal vents. Unlike earthworms, tube worms don't crawl around. They live in protective cylinders that look like huge candlesticks stuck in the ocean floor.

Nautical Nicknames

Just like people, some ocean animals have nicknames. Can you match the eight sea critters on the right with other names they are known by? Each one has a clue below it.

Nickname	Common Name
sea parrot	**albatross** Clue: *can be a bit clumsy*
unicorn of the sea	**beluga whale** Clue: *quite a singer*
sea bat	**manatee** Clue: *grazes on underwater vegetation*
clown of the sea	**lobster** Clue: *has antennae*
gooney bird	**manta ray** Clue: *has black winglike flaps*
sea cow	**common puffin** Clue: *looks like a circus character*
medusa	**narwhal whale** Clue: *has a long pointed tusk*
bug	**jellyfish** Clue: *resembles the flowing hair of a mythological creature*

FATHOM THAT! Some jellyfish can glow and flash light, like fireflies do. When it's lit up, the jellyfish suddenly looks extra big, which may frighten a predator away.

Super Squid

Whales aren't the only giants cruising the ocean! Out in the depths, squid can grow bigger than 60 feet long. Some have washed ashore, but **they are very rarely seen alive.** To find out an amazing fact about the giant squid, use the letters in the grid to fill in the empty blocks below it. Printed above and below each block are coordinates to two possible letters. To solve the puzzle, choose the correct one for each block.

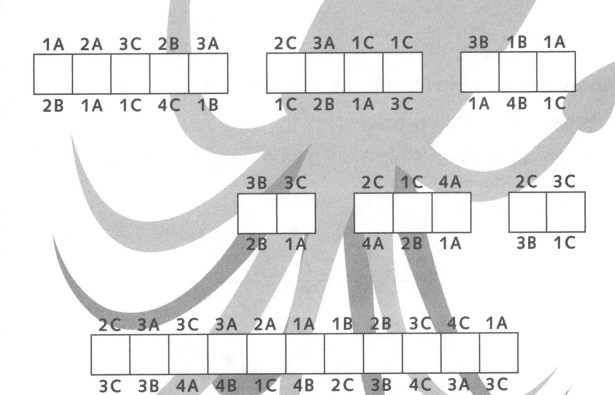

	A	B	C
1	t	r	e
2	h	i	b
3	y	a	s
4	g	k	l

1A 2A 3C 2B 3A
2B 1A 1C 4C 1B

2C 3A 1C 1C
1C 2B 1A 3C

3B 1B 1A
1A 4B 1C

3B 3C
2B 1A

2C 1C 4A
4A 2B 1A

2C 3C
3B 1C

2C 3A 3C 3A 2A 1A 1B 2B 3C 4C 1A
3C 3B 4A 4B 1C 4B 2C 3B 4C 3A 3C

Unexpected Answers

See if you can answer the following questions by replacing each letter in the solution with the letter that comes immediately before it or after it in the alphabet. For example, the letter B can be replaced with an A or a C. The solutions may surprise you!

1 What is the green sea turtle named after?

U G F   B P K N S   P G   J U T   G B S

___ ___ ___   ___ ___ ___ ___ ___   ___ ___   ___ ___ ___   ___ ___ ___

2 A lobster tastes its food with short bristles that line part of its body. What part is that?

S I D   Q H O B F Q T   B U   S G D   D O C R

___ ___ ___   ___ ___ ___ ___ ___ ___ ___   ___ ___   ___ ___ ___   ___ ___ ___ ___

N E   J S T   V B K L J M F   K D H R

___ ___   ___ ___ ___   ___ ___ ___ ___ ___ ___ ___   ___ ___ ___ ___

3 Sarcastic fringehead fish look like they're smiling, but really they tend to be pretty grouchy. When two of them battle over territory, who wins?

U G D   P O D   X H U G   S G F

___ ___ ____ ___

A J F H F R U   L P V U I

_____ _____

4 How does a starfish digest an oyster after prying open the shellfish?

C X   J O R D Q U J O F   H U T   P V M

__ _____ ___ ___

T U N L B B G   J M U N   U G D

_____ ____ ___

P Z R U D S ' R   R G F M K

_____'_ _____

Body Works

In order to **eat, breathe, and otherwise survive in salt water,** sea animals rely on parts of their bodies in different ways. See if you can correctly complete each of the statements below with one of the body parts named here.

stomach   skin   muscles
tear ducts   teeth   arms
tentacles   tail

1   A brittle star can escape from a predator by quickly dropping off and then regrowing its _____.

2   Sea turtles get rid of excess salt through their _____.

3   A sea urchin feeds on seaweed by scraping it off rocks with its five powerful _____.

4   Squid propel themselves backwards by forcing water out of their bodies with their _____.

5   Sea snakes can absorb oxygen through their _____.

6   Sea anemones catch small sea animals with their _____.

7   An otter uses a stone to break open clams on its _____.

8   The sea horse anchors itself to seaweed with its _____.

Mollusk Match

THIS ONE IS TOUGH!
Can you figure it out? Look for the upside-down clue!

Mollusks are invertebrates (animals without back-bones). Many live in a shell, but some don't. The names of nine different mollusks are in this puzzle. Some letters are already in place and the others you'll need are in the white box. Every symbol below an answer blank stands for one of the letters in the box. When you figure out what one symbol means, use it to figure out the other words.

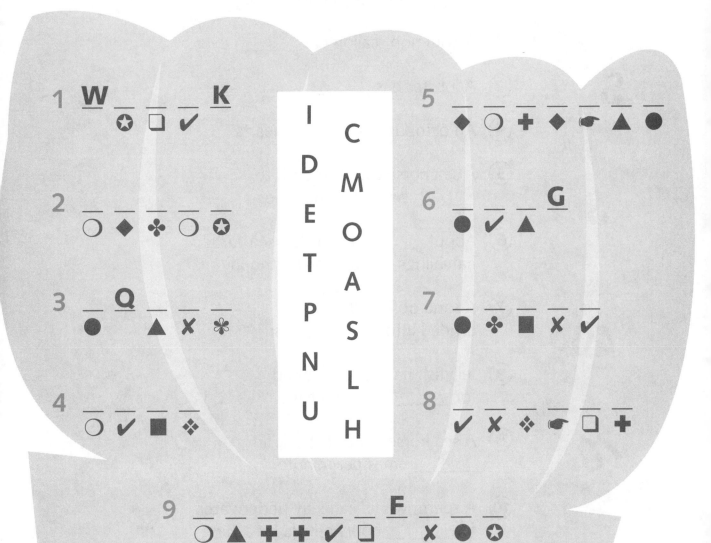

Clue: ●=S

Notable Numbers

The big numerals below are the answers to the missing **facts about sea life**. What number do you think goes in each blank?

5

8

3

400

70

(1) A newborn blue whale drinks _____ gallons of milk per day.

(2) A common scallop has _____ eyes.

(3) A lobster has _____ walking legs.

(4) An octopus has _____ hearts.

(5) A sea horse can give birth to _____ babies at one time.

(6) About _____ per 1,000 sea turtle hatchlings make it to adulthood.

(7) A sand dollar's disc is divided into _____ parts.

(8) Jellyfish have been around for _____ million years.

(9) A sea horse beats its back fin _____ times per minute.

(10) A sperm whale can stay underwater for _____ hours before breaching.

2

600

130

1

32

Briny
BRAINTEASERS
&RIDDLES

Swordfish Supper

A swordfish swam into a school of 200 mackerel and ate all but 50 of them. How many survived?

answer: 50, the ones he didn't eat

Prickly Urchin

What side of a sea urchin has more spines?

answer: the outside

Cruising Along

Why did the shark swim across the bay?

answer: for the halibut

Get In Line

Pete and Perry are two penguins from the same rookery. At the moment, Pete is standing in front of Perry, and Perry is standing in front of Pete. How is that possible?

answer: they're standing face to face

Well Suited

When a penguin has its tuxedo dry-cleaned, how does it pay the bill?

answer: with sand dollars

Going My Way?

Abby the Adelie penguin is standing directly on the South Pole facing north. If she takes one step backward, what direction will she be traveling?

answer: north, because every direction from the South Pole is north

Bait Buckets

A lobsterman has six buckets lined up on the dock. The first three are empty and the next three are full of bait. How can he make the buckets alternate between empty and full by moving only one bucket?

answer: by dumping bucket 5 into bucket 2

Clamoring for Clams

What did one crab say when the other crab ate all the clams?

answer: Don't be so shellfish!

Lots of Lobster

How many 2-pound lobsters are there in a dozen?

answer: a dozen

Under Wraps

Which marine animal is most likely to keep a secret?

Ursula the Urchin

Brenda the Butterfly Fish

Seymour the Seal

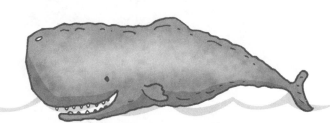

Willie the Whale

answer: Seymour the Seal, because his lips are sealed

Well Groomed

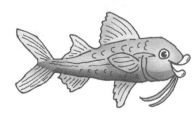

How did the goatfish shave his beard?

answer: with a razor clam

A Likely Pair

What kind of fish always seems
to show up after a pipefish?

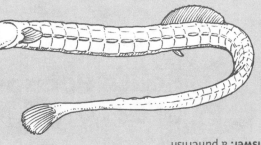

answer: a pufferfish

The Hidden Pearl

Assuming there is a pearl in just one of the oysters, and that only one of the following statements is correct, which oyster is it?

1 The pearl is in Oyster D or in Oyster A.
2 The pearl is in Oyster C or in Oyster B.
3 The pearl is in Oyster A.
4 The pearl is in Oyster B or in Oyster D.

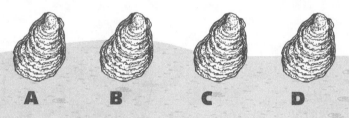

A   B   C   D

for the answer: see page 136

Welcome Committee

What did the octopus say when he noticed another octopus moving into the neighboring underwater den?

answer: Can I give you a hand, hand, hand, hand, hand, hand, hand, hand?

Petite Poisson

What do you call a baby fish from France?

Bonjour!

answer: a French fry

Snails' Pace

Every day when the tide goes out Molly and Marvin the mud snails go for a crawl across the mudflat where they live. Moving along at their slow but steady snails' pace it always takes them precisely 1 hour and 20 minutes to reach the other side. But today it took them 80 minutes! What was the difference?

answer: there is no difference; 80 minutes is 1 hour and 20 minutes

Travel Plans

Where did the sailfish spend his summer vacation?

answer: overseas

Turtle Tidings

What did the baby sea turtle say when the current swept him into the seaweed?

answer: Kelp!

Waiting Out the Storm

A fisherman cruised into port on Monday and stayed for three consecutive days to wait out a Nor'easter. He left promptly the following day, which was Monday. How could that be?

answer: the name of his boat was Monday

Market Price

What did the fisherman make on the day's catch?

answer: a net profit

Hot Pursuit

A fisherman spotted ten sharks swimming after a single tuna. What time was it?

answer: ten after one

Fishy Feat

Which fish fits on your foot?

answer: a skate

Recyclables

Can you name a sea animal that's recyclable?

answer: a bottlenose dolphin

The Mermaid's Dilemma

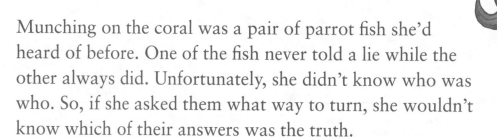

Molly the mermaid heard there were some incredible buys at the new Deep Sea Fish Market and decided to check it out. Halfway there she came to a large coral reef and didn't know whether she should go east or west.

Munching on the coral was a pair of parrot fish she'd heard of before. One of the fish never told a lie while the other always did. Unfortunately, she didn't know who was who. So, if she asked them what way to turn, she wouldn't know which of their answers was the truth.

Finally the solution dawned on Molly. In order to get the information she sought, she'd have to pose a question to just one of the fish. What is the question and how could Molly be sure of the answer?

for the answer: see page 136

Sowing Sea Seeds

What do mermaids grow in their gardens?

answer: sea lettuce and sea cucumbers

Marine Movie Production

A movie director spent the day casting the characters in his latest ocean adventure film. Who did he hire to play the roles of the marine animals?

answer: sea stars

Solo Swimmer

When does a fish swim all by itself?

answer: when it's out of school

Precious Pearls

Over the years, the oysterman's wife collected 12 pearls that she strung on a chain. Now she'd like to give each of her 12 grandchildren one of the pearls and still end up with one on the string. How can she do it?

answer: She can give eleven of her grandchildren a pearl and give one of her grandchildren a pearl on the chain

Good Fishing Spots

Where do you find the most bluefish?

answer: between its head and tail

So Long, Ray!

What did they call Stanley the stingray once the shark caught up with him?

answer: x-ray

The Curious Cuke

Sherri the Sea Cucumber was as curious as could be, always checking every new nook and cranny in the tide pool where she lived. One day she found herself in a sealed jar. Luckily she had her cell phone with her and quickly called the deep sea hotline for help. When the operator asked her what the problem was, what did she say?

answer: I think I'm in a real pickle!

Spotless Digs

Why was the octopus' cave so tidy?

answer: he hired a mermaid

Tight Squeeze

Tommy the Tuna had a quick errand to run, but when he got to his car he discovered he couldn't get out of his parking space. Why not?

answer: he was sandwiched in

Undersea Construction

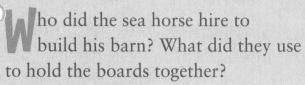

Who did the sea horse hire to build his barn? What did they use to hold the boards together?

answer: the sawfish and the hammerhead shark; they used snails

Crab Collision

Why did Sarah the Sea Horse trip over the horseshoe crab?

answer: because it was underfoot

Leaving An Impression

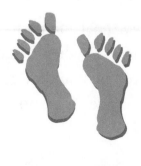

Which sea creature leaves yellow footprints on the ocean floor?

answer: a lemon sole

Deep Sea DEFINITIONS

A

Abalone
An edible mollusk with an ear-shaped shell.

Albacore
A type of tuna popular for its white meat.

Algae
Simple, nonflowering plants usually found growing in water; there are many kinds of algae, such as seaweeds.

Anemone
See: Sea Anemone.

Angel Shark
A shark with a very flat body that helps it blend in with the ocean floor.

Anglerfish
A fish that lures its prey with an appendage (body part) that looks like a fishing pole, which extends from its snout and hangs in front of its mouth.

Arthropod
A large group of invertebrates (animals without backbones) whose bodies are segmented (divided into sections) and whose skeletons are external (on the outside).

B

Baleen
A comb-like strainer that hangs like curtains in the mouths of certain whales, to filter plankton (their primary food) from the water. Baleen is made of keratin, the same stuff your fingernails are made of.

Bannerfish
A type of butterfly fish that is black, white, and yellow; it has a long fin on its back, which looks like a banner, or flag.

Barnacle
A crustacean that feeds itself by using its feathery feet to kick bits of plankton through the openings in its body.

Barracuda
A large, slender tropical fish with a toothy lower jaw that juts forward; these fish tend to be aggressive (will fight or attack).

Bed
An area of the seafloor where shellfish (such as oysters) breed.

Bivalve
A mollusk (such as an oyster or clam) whose body is enclosed within a pair of hinged shells.

Black Smokers
Chimneylike stacks formed from minerals in the hot water that blasts out of vents in the ocean floor.

Blow
The spout of spray that comes out of the hole(s) on top of a whale's head when it breathes out.

Blubber
The extra-thick body fat that helps sea animals such as seals and whales stay warm in cold ocean water.

Bluefin Tuna
A large tuna that is an important source of food for humans.

Blue Marlin
A large fish with a pointed upper bill that looks like a short sword; this fish lives in the open sea and can grow up to weigh 1,000 pounds or more.

Bouillabaisse
A kind of fish stew from France.

Brittle Star
This relative of the sea star has long, flexible, spiny arms; as with other starfish, if an arm is broken off, it will grow back.

Buoy
A float that is anchored and marks something that is under the water, such as a reef, a lobster trap, or a boat mooring.

Butterfly Fish
A type of warm-water reef fish with a compressed (narrow) body that is brightly colored and boldly marked.

C

Calf
A young whale.

Canopy
A cloth or canvas stretched over an overhead frame, which provides shelter from the sun.

Chick
A young penguin.

Cephalopod
Generally, a fast-swimming mollusk, such as an octopus, cuttlefish, or squid.

Clown Fish
A small tropical fish with bold stripes (typically orange and white); also known as an anemone fish, it is immune to the stings of sea anemones (unlike most other fish).

Cod
A large fish that is caught for food, and is also a good source of oil (cod-liver oil).

Conch
A tropical (warm-water) marine mollusk with a large spiral shell.

Cone Snail
A tropical (warm-water) marine mollusk with a shell shaped like a cone; it stuns or kills its prey with poison.

Coral Reefs
Undersea structures formed by the skeletons of countless coral polyps. See Polyp.

Cormorant
A dark-colored diving bird with a long neck, a hooked bill, and a big appetite.

Crustacean
A diverse (different from one another) group of arthropods (such as crabs, lobsters, krill, and shrimps), most of which live in water and have four or more pairs of limbs.

Currents
Huge streams of moving water that travel through and around the oceans.

Cuttlefish

A mollusk that belongs to the same group as octopuses and squid; it can disguise itself when sneaking up on its prey by changing the color of its skin.

D

Damselfish

A small, brilliantly-colored, tropical (warm-water) marine fish that lives in coral reefs.

Dilemma

A situation or problem in which you must choose between two or more possibilities.

Dogfish

A small shark with a long tail; the spiny dogfish is the most common shark.

Dolphin

A small, friendly toothed whale that has a curved fin on its back and a beaklike snout.

Dottyback

A brightly-colored fish that feeds on small crustaceans.

Dugong

A mammal that resembles a manatee but has a forked tail; it lives in the shallow coastal waters of the Indian Ocean.

E

Eel

A type of fish with a snakelike shape.

Elephant Fish

A silvery white fish with a hoe-shaped snout; it lives near the coasts of southern Australia and New Zealand.

Elver

A young eel.

Ephyna

A young jellyfish.

Escargot

Originally a French dish, this refers to snails prepared in restaurants for food.

F

Fathom
To understand; or to measure the depth of water. A fathom is equal to six feet of water.

Flipper
A broad flat limb that certain sea animals (such as seals, whales, and turtles) use to swim.

Flounder
A small flatfish that usually moves horizontally (like a rug) along the ocean floor.

Fry
A young fish.

G

Gastropod
Mollusks, such as a snail, that have a large muscular foot for moving around and live in a single spiral shell (or in no shell).

Gills
Thin flaps of body tissue used by fish to absorb oxygen out of the water, allowing them to breathe underwater.

Goatfish
A fish that uses the barbels (fleshy threadlike growths) on its chin to stir up the ocean floor to find food.

Goby
A kind of small fish found in tide-pools, oyster beds, and mudflats.

Grouper
A member of the sea bass fish family; groupers can be recognized by their big heads and mouths.

Grunt
A tropical (warm-water) fish related to the snapper but with fewer teeth and usually smaller.

Guitarfish
A type of ray that resembles a guitar, with its roundish body and wide tail.

Gull

A seabird that has long wings, webbed feet, a loud call, and plumage (feathers) that is typically white and gray or black.

H

Halibut

A large-mouth flatfish that is a member of the flounder group.

Hatchetfish

A silvery deep-sea fish shaped like a hatchet blade; it has organs that light up along its stomach and tail.

Hatchling

A young animal (such as a sea turtle) that has recently come out of its egg.

Herring

A fish that lives in the Atlantic and Pacific oceans which is an important source of food for bigger fish as well as for humans.

Hydrothermal Vents

Hot water springs found deep down on the ocean floor, where water that seeps down to the earth's inner layer is heated up to super-hot temperatures.

I

Invertebrate

An animal that doesn't have a backbone.

Isopod

A crustacean with a flat segmented body.

J

Jawfish

A small fish with a long jaw.

K

Kelp

A large brown seaweed with a long, strong stipe (stem) and broad blades (leaves); some kelp grows into huge undersea "forests" that provide a home for many marine animals.

Krill

Tiny shrimplike animals that whales and penguins love to eat.

L

Limpet
A marine mollusk with a single shell and a wide foot, which it uses to cling to rocks.

Lionfish
A fish found in the Indian and Pacific oceans that has hollow, poisonous spines that resemble a lion's mane.

M

Mackerel
A swift, sleek fish with a deeply forked tail.

Mammal
A warm-blooded vertebrate (animal with a backbone) that has hair or fur, produces milk for its young, and usually gives birth to live young (rather than laying eggs).

Manatee
A mammal with a rounded tail flipper that lives in the shallow coastal waters and connecting rivers in tropical areas of the Atlantic Ocean.

Marine
Something that is found in, or comes from, the sea.

Marine Iguana
A type of lizard that swims in the ocean; iguanas are found on the Galapagos Islands in the Pacific and off the coast of Ecuador in South America.

Medusa
A free-swimming bell- or disk-shaped creature with tentacles and a mouth on its underside (such as a jellyfish).

Melon
A waxy mass or mound in the head of a dolphin or other toothed whales.

Menagerie
A collection of animals on exhibit (display).

Mermaid
A fictional or mythical (not real) sea creature that has the head

and upper body of a woman and the tail of a fish.

Mollusk
An invertebrate (animal without a backbone) with a soft body, such as a clam, that is usually, but not always, enclosed in a shell.

Mussel
A type of shellfish that attaches itself to rocks at the low tide line, where it filters plankton from the water flowing over it.

O

Olive Snail
A type of marine snail with a smooth, shiny shell shaped like an olive.

Orca
A large, toothed whale with black and white markings; it is also referred to as a killer whale.

Osprey
A large fish-eating bird also known as a fish hawk.

P

Parrot Fish
A tropical (warm-water) fish with a beaklike mouth and fused (joined together) teeth for munching on coral.

Pearl
A shiny sphere or ball formed when certain shellfish (such as oysters) cover a grain of sand or other object with layers of mother-of-pearl, the same substance that forms the inside of their shells.

Pelican
A waterbird with a long bill and a pouch in its throat for catching fish.

Periwinkle
A small marine snail with a thick, coiled shell, which is often collected and eaten by people.

Pickleweed
A plant that can grow in wet, salty marshes and flats where other plants can't grow.

Pincer
The claw of a lobster, crab, or certain other crustaceans, used to grasp food.

Pinniped
A group of large marine mammals that includes seals, sea lions, and walruses.

Pipefish
A skinny fish that can grow to about a foot long, has a long snout, and usually lives in shallow water.

Plankton
Small and microscopic animals, plants, and single-cell life-forms that are found floating in ocean waters.

Pod
A small herd of whales.

Poisson
The French word for fish.

Polyp
The living part of coral, which forms a protective, cuplike home; coral reefs are formed as new polyps build on top of the skeletons of old polyps that have died off.

Porbeagle
A big stout (thick and heavy) shark that lives in cold water; related to the mako and great white shark.

Porpoise
A small, toothed whale that has a short triangular fin on its back and a blunt (rounded rather than pointed) snout.

Predator
An animal that hunts and feeds on another animal.

Prey
An animal that is hunted and eaten by another animal.

Puffer
A fish that can inflate (blow up) its body with air or water in order to look bigger and therefore more scary to its predators.

Pup
A name that refers to the young of some mammals, including an otter.

Pursuit
The act of following or chasing something.

R

Raft
A group of otters.

Rattail
A deep-sea fish with a big head and body and a tapering tail (thins down toward the end).

Ray
A broad, flat marine fish with a skeleton made of cartilage (firm but flexible tissue), fins shaped like wings, and a long slender tail.

Recyclable
An object or substance (material) that can be used again.

Reptile
A cold-blooded vertebrate (animal with a backbone) that has scaly skin and usually lays eggs to produce young.

Rookery
A colony of breeding seabirds (such as penguins), seals, or turtles.

S

Sailfish
A fish with a pointed bill and a tall, sail-like fin on its back.

Sarcastic Fringehead
A fish that looks like it's smiling but actually is not very good-natured.

Sardine
A silvery fish that is a member of the herring family.

Sawfish
A sharklike ray with a nose that looks like a saw.

Scampi
An Italian dish of shrimps, cooked in garlic and butter.

School
A large
group of fish.

Scorpionfish
A fish with poisonous
spines, which lives near
the ocean bottom.

Sea Anemone
A sea animal that looks like a
flower and attaches itself to the
ocean floor (although it does
move around a bit); prey is stung
and captured with a ring of
tentacles around its mouth.

Sea Cucumber
A sausage-shaped marine animal
that is related to sea stars and
urchins.

Sea Dragon
A marine animal related to the
sea horse and pipefish; it moves
through the water like floating
seaweed.

Sea Fan
A type of coral that's shaped like
a fan and anchors itself to the
ocean floor.

Sea Slug
A shell-less marine animal related
to the slugs found in your
garden.

Sea Sponge
A primitive animal that filters
food from the water that flows
through the many holes in its
body.

Sea Star
A marine invertebrate (animal
without a backbone), also
known as a starfish, with a thick,
central body from which five or
more arms extend (stick out).

Sea Urchin
A marine animal, related to the
sand dollar, that is covered with
prickly spines that resemble a
porcupine's.

Sea Wasp
A box-shaped jellyfish with a
dangerous sting.

Skate
A marine fish of the ray family.

Smack
A group of jellyfish.

Snapper
A tropical fish named for the way it snaps its toothed jaws.

Sole
A marine flatfish found around the world.

Spat
A young oyster.

Species
A group of similar animals in which the individuals can mate with one another; crabeater and leopard, for example, are two species of seals.

Sushi
A Japanese dish made with rice, raw fish, and vegetables.

Swarm
A group of eels.

T ....

Tentacle
A long, flexible limb usually found near the mouth of an animal, such as a squid, and used for grasping food or moving around.

Tern
A seabird with long pointed wings and a forked tail; it is related to the gull but is usually smaller and not as plump.

Tidepool
A small saltwater pond that forms along rocky coastlines and is home to many interesting sea creatures.

Trevally
A fish of the Indian Ocean and nearby Pacific Ocean; it is caught in large quantities for food.

Tube Worms
Giant worms that live in tubes protruding from (sticking out of) the ocean floor around hydrothermal vents.

U ....

Univalve
An animal (such as a snail) that has only one shell.

V

Viperfish
A small, long fish with fangs, which lives in the deep sea.

W

Whale
See pages 113 and 114.

Whelk
A marine mollusk with a pointed spiral shell.

Wrasse
Pretty tropical (warm-water) fish with big teeth, a small mouth, and large, smooth scales.

A Ton of Whales

Whales come in many shapes and sizes, but there are only two major groups of whales: baleen and toothed. Here are some more facts about these amazing marine animals!

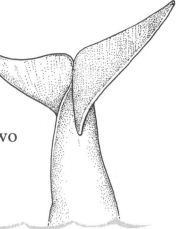

Baleen Whales

Blue whales are the largest animals on the planet, measuring up to 100 feet or longer. Blue whale calves grow quickly, gaining up to 200 pounds a day when they're nursing.

Bowhead whales often feed by swimming along the surface of the water with their mouths open, trapping food in their baleen—a practice known as skimming. Their baleen is relatively long compared to other whales, and they tend to have a high percentage of blubber for their body weight.

Fin whales are one of the fastest large whales, swimming up to 35 miles or so per hour. Their heads are triangular in shape and their bodies tend to be dark on top and white underneath.

Gray whales feed on crustaceans by sucking up sediment from the ocean floor, then filtering dirt and other debris out of their mouths through their baleen.

Minke whales are small and smooth, resembling dolphins with tall fins on their backs. They tend to feed on a wider assortment of fish than other whales.

Pygmy whales are the smallest of the baleen whales. They are found in the warmer waters of the southern hemisphere but sightings of them are considered rare.

Right whales have hardened patches of skin on their head, plump bodies, and no fins on their backs.

Sei whales eat a variety of other sea animals, including fish and squid, although they mostly feed on plankton strained from the water with their unusually fine baleen. They have sleek bodies with tall, pointed back fins.

Toothed Whales

Beluga whales, also called white whales, are born dark gray and have no back fins. They turn white as they become adults. Belugas tend to be very vocal, a trait that has led to them being called the canaries of the sea.

Hourglass dolphins are pretty, black-and-white dolphins (dolphins are small, toothed whales). They live in the Antarctic waters and are rarely seen near land.

Humpback whales have flippers that are longer than those of other whales, and the undersides of their tails are marked with unique black-and-white skin patterns.

Killer whales, also called Orcas, use their teeth to catch lots of different kinds of prey, including fish, squid, penguins, and sea lions. Orcas have striking black-and-white bodies.

Melon-headed whales are small with a thin body and a head that is pointed and shaped somewhat like a melon. They are fast swimmers and prey mostly on small fish and squid.

Narwhal whales resemble the mythical unicorn — this species has a long, pointed tusk protruding from its head. Its skin is colored with flecks of brown and gray.

Pilot whales tend to swim in large groups and feed mostly on squid. There are two types: the long-finned type, which is usually found in cold waters, and the short-finned type, which inhabits warmer waters.

Sperm whales feed on squid and can dive to amazing depths to find them. They have huge square heads, like the famous sperm whale Moby Dick.

Salty
SOLUTIONS

Page 2 — Double-Talk

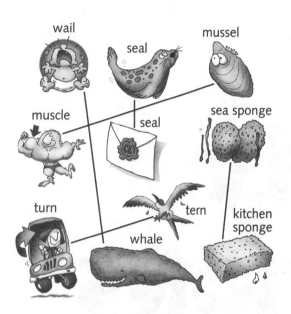

wail
seal
mussel
muscle
seal
sea sponge
turn
tern
whale
kitchen sponge

Page 3 — Marine Menagerie

Page 4–5 — Seafood Sampler

1. fried clams
2. sushi
3. clam chowder
4. escargot
5. broiled scallops
6. fish and chips
7. bouillabaisse
8. steamers
9. oyster stew
10. shrimp scampi

Page 6–7 — Telling Tails

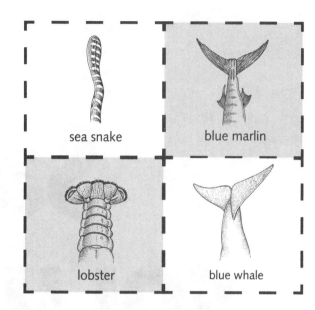

sea snake

blue marlin

lobster

blue whale

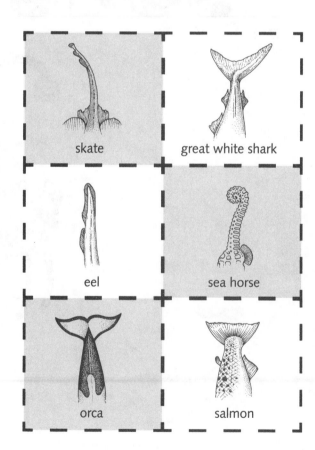

skate

great white shark

eel

sea horse

orca

salmon

Page 8 — Are You In My Class?

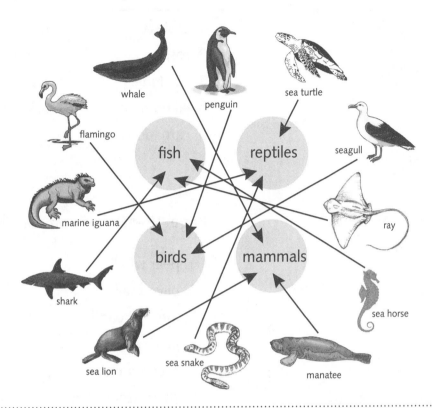

Page 9 — Seaside Charades

1. shellfish
2. pilot whale
3. bed of oysters
4. sea lion
5. happy as a clam
6. horseshoe crab

Page 10 — Whale Words

1. flippers
2. pod
3. blow
4. melon
5. calf

Page 11 — Creature Feature

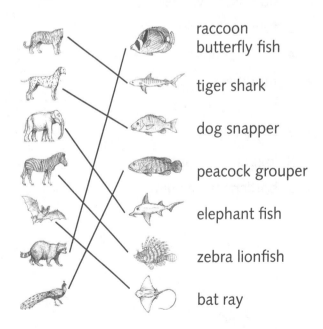

raccoon
butterfly fish

tiger shark

dog snapper

peacock grouper

elephant fish

zebra lionfish

bat ray

Page 12–13 — Spineless Sea Creatures

1. comb jelly

   apple anemone

   star coral

2. pencil urchin

   basket star

   pancake sand dollar

3. sea lemon

   broadclub cuttlefish

   weathervane scallop

4. slipper lobster

   acorn barnacle

   horseshoe crab

Page 14–15 — Bodybuilding

1. donkey's ear abalone
2. humpback whale
3. foureye butterfly fish
4. finger sponge
5. thornback ray
6. brain coral
7. spiny urchin
8. loggerhead turtle
9. bottlenose dolphin

Page 16–17 — Coral Collection

1. table
2. rose
3. sea fan
4. elkhorn
5. carnation
6. fire
7. elephant ears
8. organ pipes
9. brain

Page 18–19 — Food for Thought

1. pear whelk
2. olive snail
3. melon-head whale
4. pickleweed
5. coconut crab
6. cherrystone clam
7. peppermint shrimp
8. lettuce sea slug
9. apple anemone
10. lemon shark
11. chocolate chip star
12. sea cucumber

Page 22 — Sea Sounds

1. penguin
2. dolphin
3. dugong
4. porpoise
5. starfish
6. stingray

Bonus Question: dugong

Page 20–21 — Guess That Gastropod

1. giant button top
2. butterfly moon snail
3. tent olive
4. chickpea cowrie
5. Florida worm shell
6. ladder cone
7. lightning whelk
8. king helmet
9. chestnut turban

Page 23 — What's the Word?

1. bell
2. limestone
3. spines
4. funnel
5. whiskers
6. bladder

Page 24 — Which Whale?

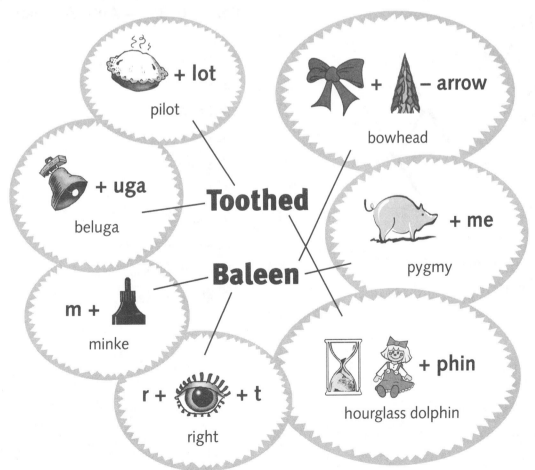

+ lot
pilot

+ uga
beluga

m +
minke

r + + t
right

+ – arrow
bowhead

+ me
pygmy

+ phin
hourglass dolphin

Toothed

Baleen

Page 26 — The Hungry Gulls

Believe it or not, both flounders are exactly the same size. If you want to see for yourself, measure them with a ruler. The narrowness of the far end of the pier creates the illusion that the fish at that end is bigger.

Page 28 — Flip-Flop Fish

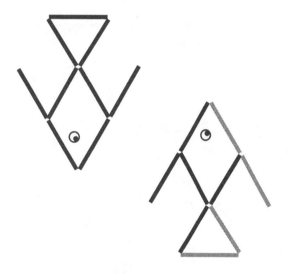

━━━━ stays where it is
━━━━ gets moved

Page 29 — See Birds

1. puffin
2. gull
3. tern
4. penguin
5. cormorant
6. osprey
7. pelican
8. dodo

Mystery Bird: Dodo

Page 30–31 — Auto Animals

1. salmon
2. sea star
3. I'm an eel
4. tuna
5. skate
6. two claws (lobster)
7. manatee
8. sea anemone
9. eight arms (octopus)
10. elephant seal

Page 27 — Prey Way

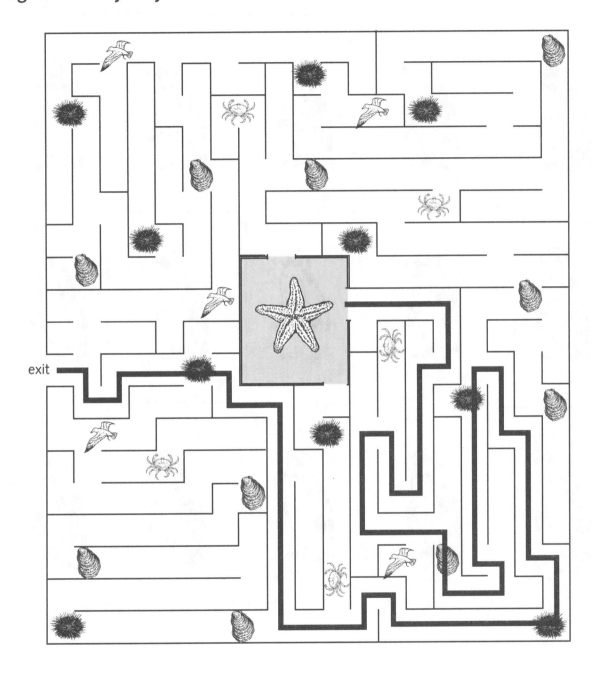

exit

Page 33 — Well Armed

The missing symbol is **OO**
The octopus is hunting for scallops

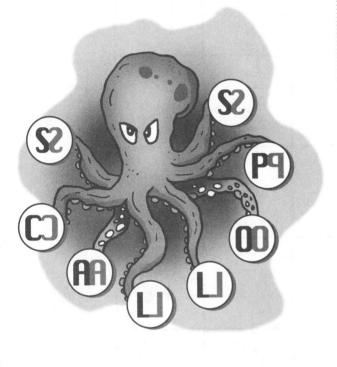

Page 34 — Sardine School

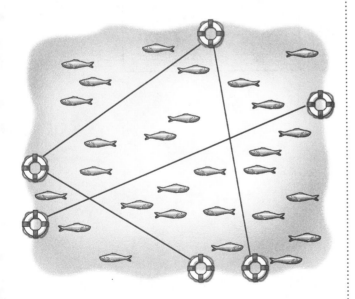

Page 36–37 — One Fish, Two Fish

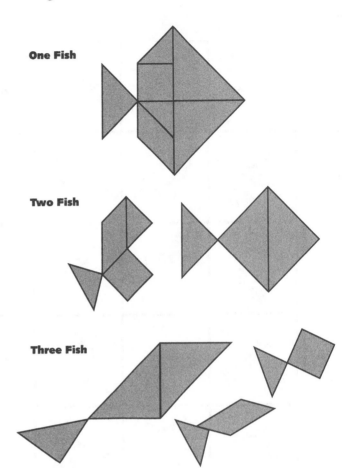

One Fish

Two Fish

Three Fish

Page 35 — Crustacean Cubes

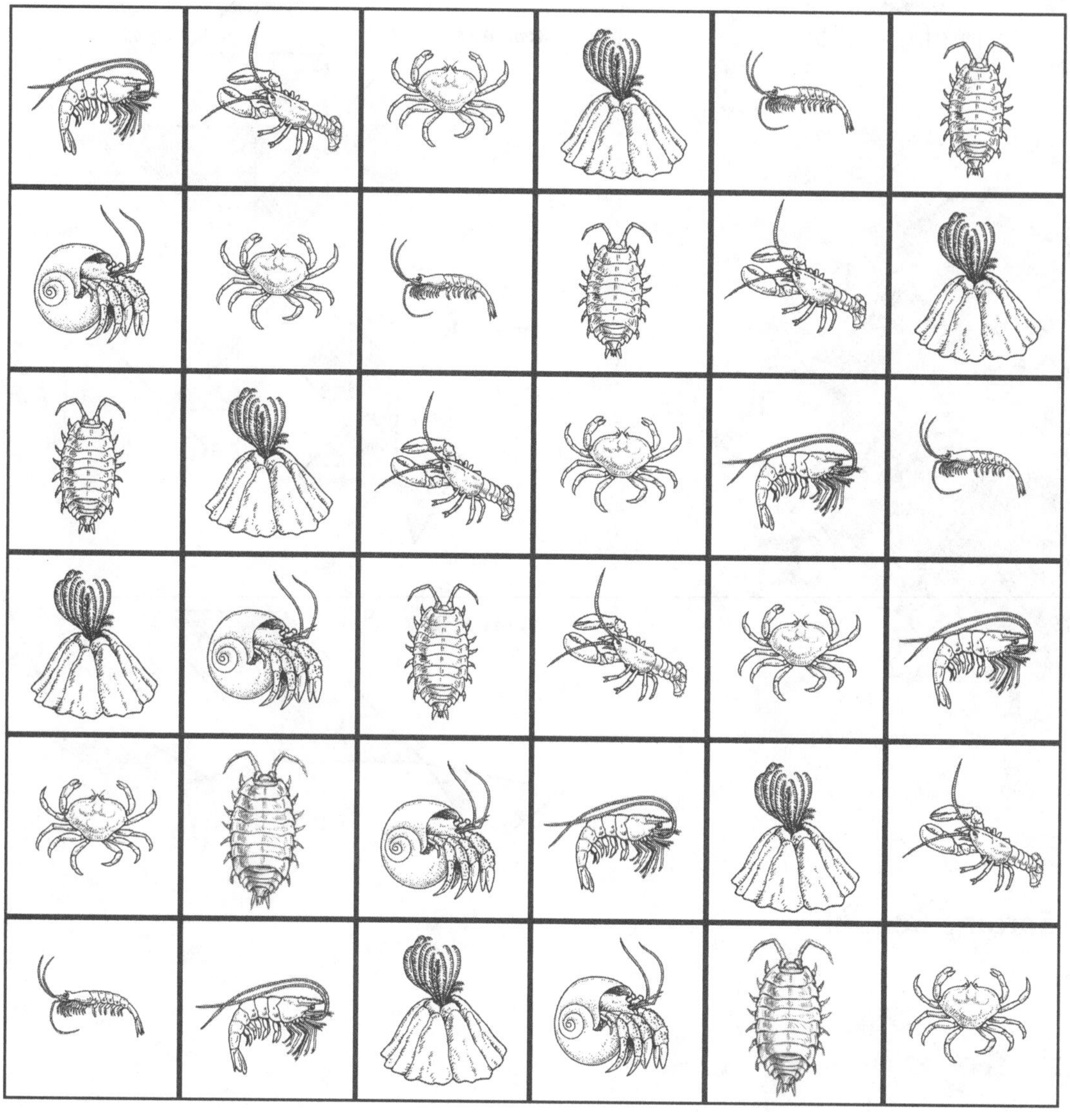

Page 38 — Marine All-Stars

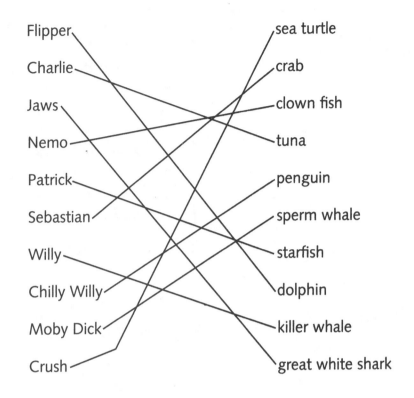

Flipper — dolphin

Charlie — tuna

Jaws — great white shark

Nemo — clown fish

Patrick — starfish

Sebastian — crab

Willy — killer whale

Chilly Willy — penguin

Moby Dick — sperm whale

Crush — sea turtle

Page 39 — The Diving Otter

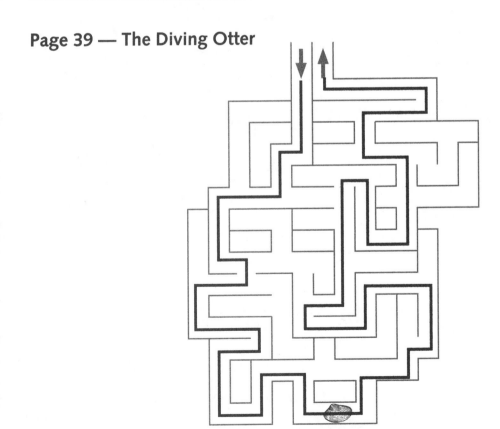

Page 40–41 — Catch the Drift

1. lobster roll
2. plenty of fish in the sea
3. flounder around
4. striped bass
5. seven seas
6. crosscurrents
7. circling sharks
8. fish out of water
9. deep sea
10. breaking wave
11. rising tide
12. swimming against the tide

Page 42 — Swift Swimmers

1st Place – sailfish
2nd Place – bluefin tuna
3rd Place – dolphin
4th Place – orca
5th Place – penguin
6th Place – human
7th Place – sea horse

Page 44 — Tidepool Tally

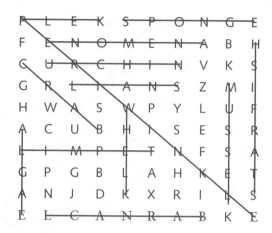

Page 45 — Deep-Sea Circles

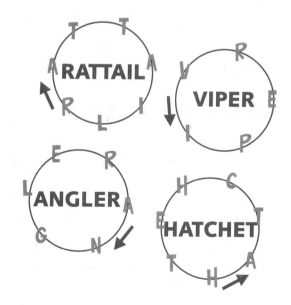

Page 46 — Better Letters

1. snail
2. lobster
3. krill
4. otter
5. shrimp
6. clam
7. cod
8. gull
9. bass
10. seal
11. sea jelly
12. sand dollar
13. nurse shark
14. moray eel
15. blue crab
16. sea slug
17. sea fan
18. killer whale
19. sea lion
20. sea star

Page 47 — Name It

1. halibut
2. stingray
3. bannerfish
4. rose coral
5. jellyfish
6. mackerel
7. trevally
8. dottyback
9. angel shark
10. blue marlin

Pages 48–49 — Who's Who Clues

1. shark
2. snail
3. sardine
4. seal
5. whale
6. otter
7. squid
8. krill

Page 50 — Shark Scramble

1. tiger
2. mako
3. blue
4. whale
5. basking
6. nurse
7. hammerhead
8. lemon
9. great white
10. leopard
11. sandbar
12. porbeagle

Page 51 — Sea What I Mean?

1. as happy as a clam
2. clam up
3. fish out of water
4. a whale of an appetite
5. flounder around

Sea Saying: SOUNDS FISHY TO ME

Page 52 — Loggerhead Lunch

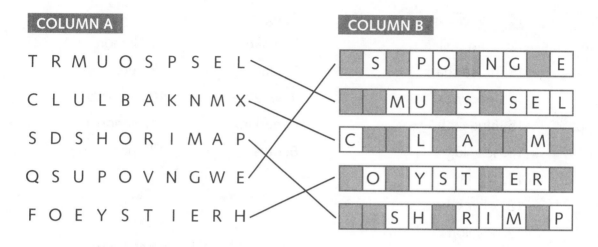

COLUMN A

T R M U O S P S E L

C L U L B A K N M X

S D S H O R I M A P

Q S U P O V N G W E

F O E Y S T I E R H

COLUMN B

S P O N G E

M U S S E L

C L A M

O Y S T E R

S H R I M P

What's Different? ~~P~~ S ~~L~~ O ~~P~~ F ~~R~~ T ~~K~~ = SOFT

Page 53 — Team Up

BABY	COMMON NAME	GROUP
fry	FISH	pod
pup	EEL	smack
spat	JELLYFISH	rookery
elver	OTTER	school
ephyna	OYSTER	bed
calf	PENGUIN	swarm
chick	WHALE	raft

Pages 54–55 — Wacky Rhyme Time

1. eel wheel
2. fish dish
3. clam jam
4. snail trail
5. seal meal
6. dull gull
7. great skate
8. squid lid
9. whale tale
10. shark ark
11. lunar tuna
12. manatee canopy

Page 56 — Fish Find

```
G  G  N  I  R  R  E  H  R        G  G  N  I  R  R  E  H  R
O  Y  S  A  S  N  L  E  E        O  Y  S  A  S  N  L  E  E
A  B  Y  N  I  C  D  H  S        A  B  Y  N  I  C  D  H  S
T  O  C  D  A  N  U  T  S        T  O  C  D  A  N  U  T  S
F  G  R  O  U  P  E  R  A        F  G  R  O  U  P  E  R  A
I  A  O  O  D  O  P  L  R        I  A  O  O  D  O  P  L  R
S  A  L  M  O  N  S  E  W        S  A  L  M  O  N  S  E  W
H  F  R  E  F  F  U  P  R        H  F  R  E  F  F  U  P  R
B  A  S  S  T  N  U  R  G        B  A  S  S  T  N  U  R  G


G  G  N  I  R  R  E  H  R        G  G  N  I  R  R  E  H  R
O  Y  S  A  S  N  L  E  E        O  Y  S  A  S  N  L  E  E
A  B  Y  N  I  C  D  H  S        A  B  Y  N  I  C  D  H  S
T  O  C  D  A  N  U  T  S        T  O  C  D  A  N  U  T  S
F  G  R  O  U  P  E  R  A        F  G  R  O  U  P  E  R  A
I  A  O  O  D  O  P  L  R        I  A  O  O  D  O  P  L  R
S  A  L  M  O  N  S  E  W        S  A  L  M  O  N  S  E  W
H  F  R  E  F  F  U  P  R        H  F  R  E  F  F  U  P  R
B  A  S  S  T  N  U  R  G        B  A  S  S  T  N  U  R  G
```

BONUS ANSWER: SCHOOLS

```
G  G  N  I  R  R  E  H  R
O  Y  S  A  S  N  L  E  E
A  B  Y  N  I  C  D  H  S
T  O  C  D  A  N  U  T  S
F  G  R  O  U  P  E  R  A
I  A  O  O  D  O  P  L  R
S  A  L  M  O  N  S  E  W
H  F  R  E  F  F  U  P  R
B  A  S  S  T  N  U  R  G
```

Page 57 — It's a Fact

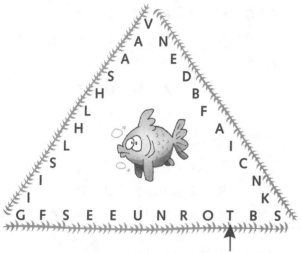

start here and go around clockwise

Answer: TRUE FISH HAVE BACKBONES, GILLS, AND FINS.

Page 59 — Sea Jelly Jazz

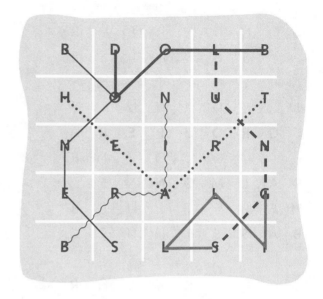

~~~ BRAIN   —— GILLS

—— BLOOD   - - LUNGS

—— BONES   ······ HEART

Page 58 — Hue Are You?

1. yellowlip parrot fish
2. great white shark
3. blue-ringed octopus
4. pink salmon or red salmon
5. red spiny sea urchin
6. green moray eel
7. green turtle
8. yellow head jawfish
9. blue whale, gray whale or white whale
10. yellow pencil coral
11. black-speckled brittle star
12. yellow-bellied sea snake

Page 60–61 — That Stings!

1. stingray
2. sea anemone
3. jellyfish
4. sea wasp
5. scorpion fish
6. brain coral
7. sea urchin

Stinging Features: tentacles or spines

Page 62 — Shuffle Squares

Block 4	Block 6	Block 2	Block 1	Block 3	Block 6

S	T	I	N	G	R	A	Y	S		A	R	E		W	H	A	T
H	A	M	M	E	R	H	E	A	D		S	H	A	R	K	S	
L	I	K	E		T	O		E	A	T		B	E	S	T		

Page 63 — Salty City

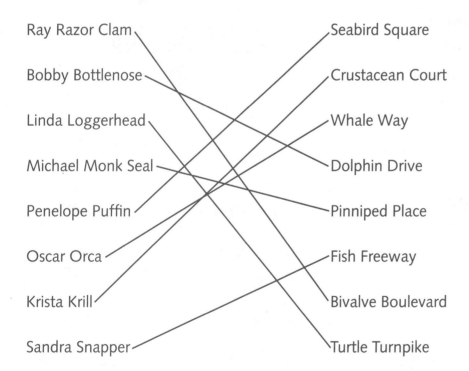

Ray Razor Clam — Crustacean Court

Bobby Bottlenose — Dolphin Drive

Linda Loggerhead — Bivalve Boulevard

Michael Monk Seal — Pinniped Place

Penelope Puffin — Seabird Square

Oscar Orca — Whale Way

Krista Krill — Fish Freeway

Sandra Snapper — Turtle Turnpike

Page 64–65 — Sea-ing Double

1. barracuda
2. butterfly fish
3. parrot fish
4. manatee
5. brittle star
6. jellyfish
7. sand dollar
8. otter
9. fiddler crab
10. loggerhead turtle

Page 66 — What Do You Call a Fish?

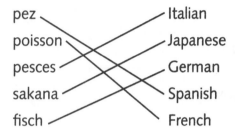

pez — Spanish
poisson — French
pesces — Italian
sakana — Japanese
fisch — German

Page 66 — Distant Shores

1. Portuguese man-o-war
2. French grunt
3. Mexican hogfish
4. Alaskan king crab
5. American eel
6. Norwegian lobster
7. African penguin
8. China moon snail

Page 67 — Clam Up

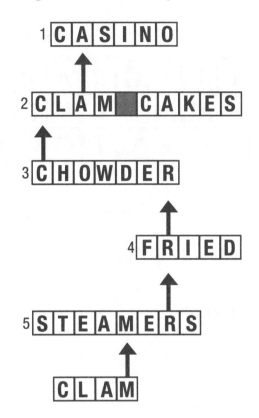

1 CASINO
2 CLAM CAKES
3 CHOWDER
4 FRIED
5 STEAMERS
CLAM

Page 68–69 — You're Hired!

The Carpentry Crew
hammerhead shark
sawfish
plankton
hatchetfish

The Fairy-Tale Characters
damselfish
sea dragon
wolf eel

The Circus Performers
clown fish
lionfish
elephant seal
sea horse

The Group of Musicians
organpipe coral
fiddler crab
guitarfish
harp seal

Page 70 — In a Word

1. manatee
2. dolphin
3. sea horse
4. octopus
5. pelican
6. sailfish
7. leatherback
8. clown fish
9. flounder
10. stingray

Page 74 — Four of a Kind

1. lobster
2. crab
3. coral
4. shark
5. urchin
6. salmon
7. shrimp
8. seal
9. whale
10. penguin

Page 76–77 — Undersea Sculptures

Page 71 — Feeding Frenzy

Page 75 — Seaweed for Lunch?

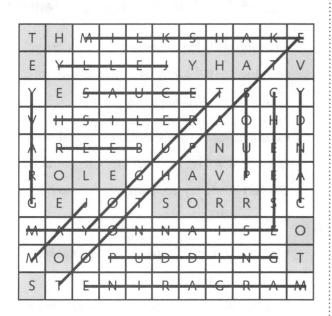

Fact: THEY HAVE NO LEAVES OR ROOTS.

Page 78 — Nautical Nicknames

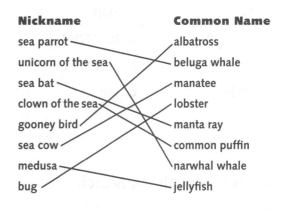

Page 79 — Super Squid

2C	3A	3C	3A	2A	1A	1B	2B	3C	4C	1A
B	A	S	K	E	T	B	A	L	L	S
3C	3B	4A	4B	1C	4B	2C	3B	4C	3A	3C

Page 80–81 — Unexpected Answers

1. the color of its fat
2. the pincers at the ends of its walking legs
3. the one with the biggest mouth
4. by inserting its own stomach into the oyster's shell

Page 82 — Body Works

1. arms
2. tear ducts
3. teeth
4. muscles
5. skin
6. tentacles
7. stomach
8. tail

Page 83 — Mollusk Match

1. whelk
2. conch
3. squid
4. clam
5. octopus
6. slug
7. snail
8. limpet
9. cuttlefish

Page 84 — Notable Numbers

1. 130 gallons of milk
2. 32 eyes
3. 8 walking legs
4. 3 hearts
5. 400 babies
6. 1 sea turtle hatchling
7. 5 parts
8. 600 million years
9. 70 times per minute
10. 2 hours

Page 90 — The Hidden Pearl

The pearl is in Oyster C. Here's why:

• If the pearl were in Oyster A, then both statements 1 and 3 would be true. Since only one statement can be right, neither 1 nor 3 can be correct. So, the pearl can't be in Oyster A.

• If the pearl were in Oyster B, then both statements 2 and 4 would be true. So, the pearl can't be in Oyster B.

• Likewise, Oyster D isn't a possibility because that would make both statements 1 and 4 true.

• That leaves Oyster C as the only possibility.

Page 94 — The Mermaid's Dilemma

All Molly needs to do is ask either parrot fish what the OTHER parrot fish would answer to her question, "Should I go east or west?"

• If the parrot fish she asks is the one that never tells a lie, it will tell her what the other parrot fish (the liar) would say; so, the answer would be the wrong direction.

• If the parrot fish she asks is the one that lies, it will lie about what the honest fish would say. So once again, the answer would be the wrong direction.

With either fish, if the answer Molly is given is east, the correct direction would be west; if the answer is west, she should head east.